THE CLOSEST THING TO MAGIC

Andrea Hogan

The Closest Thing to Magic

Published by Spines

ISBN: 979-8-90002-294-9

Spines

THE CLOSEST THING TO MAGIC

The Camino de Santiago: Through My Mother's Forgetting and My Own Becoming

ANDREA HOGAN

"Longest way around is the shortest way home,"
James Joyce, in Ulysses.

DEDICATION

For Mum, who lit and inspired the path long before I walked it.
For my sister Barbara, Mum's archangel, guiding her through the hardest transitions with grace.
For Neil, my husband, whose love and steady support gave me the freedom to take this journey.
For Jordan and Ryan, who love me, challenge me, and make me want to be better every day.
And for my Camino friends, thank you for the laughter, the stories, and every step we shared along the way.

CONTENTS

PROLOGUE

THE LOVELY LONENESS

Mum's Camino entry, Santiago, Sept 25th, 2012.

"It's so much fun; sometimes I forget to look around at the stunning scenery. It's the second-to-last day. I want to see Santiago. I have walked nearly 850 km in its direction, always seeing the spires in my mind's eye. I just don't want the fun with the crowd to end. I don't want the lovely loneliness—while not being alone—to end."

My mother had walked this path at sixty-eight, with no plan and only a backpack, chasing something of her own. She called it "the greatest adventure of her life." Exactly twelve years later, I stood at the same starting line, carrying not only my own pack but the weight of her fading story. By then, Alzheimer's had begun quietly unspooling her story, one thread at a time. I came to Spain not only to grieve what was slipping away, but to follow the echoes of her footsteps — and maybe, along the way, find the pieces of her I never fully knew.

Losing her felt like losing the very map of myself, as if

my own memory were being erased—the memory of how I made sense of the world. My mother wasn't just a presence in my life; she was my compass, my confidante, my person. We spoke every day, about everything and nothing, and in those conversations, she stitched meaning and steadiness into my days. She was my sounding board, the voice that made the world less confusing and more bearable. As Alzheimer's slowly took her away, it felt as though the foundation of my own memory and understanding cracked beneath me. To lose her was not only to lose the woman I adored but also the anchor who helped me locate myself in the vastness of life.

We had roamed the world together — Paris, London, Aspen, New York, Las Vegas, Yosemite, Chicago, Prague, Berlin, Los Angeles — collecting adventures as if they might ward off time itself. Although I was so grateful for them, I wasn't ready for them to end. This Camino became my chance to have one last journey with her: her words alive on paper, her voice echoing in my head. With every step, I carried her beside me and, slowly, very slowly, learned to accept that she was slipping further away. The walk gave me the space not only to honor her, but to process the ache of losing her — as she, in her illness, was also losing me.

I remember years earlier when my mother stood over her own mother's grave. She wept in a way I had never seen before, and through her sobs, she whispered, "I am no one's baby anymore." Something broke inside me. Through those four words, I understood the depth of her loss. And now, on the Camino, I felt the same dread blooming in me. I wasn't ready to stop being her baby. No one advises you, scolds you, or lifts you quite like a mother does. That role is sacred, and I already missed her — even though she was still here.

This book insisted on being written. Not as a vanity project, but as an act of devotion from a daughter to a mother she loves—a way to capture both her story and mine before time could quietly blur the edges. As I reread our words, side by side, I didn't just remember the Camino—I reentered it. I felt the magic of that ancient path stir once more, a quiet alchemy that now binds us both. A magic that remains, even as she gently slips beyond reach.

Woven through these pages are the twin narratives of our pilgrimages: mine, recorded in the daily entries I scribbled into my journal; hers, drawn from the modest copybook she carried on her second attempt, beginning in Logroño.

The Camino is not just a walk. It strips you down—layer by layer—until all you have left is your truest self, your aching feet, and whatever you're carrying in your heart. Somewhere along those miles, in searching for the pieces of her story, I would begin to stitch together my own. The Camino didn't just give me back fragments of her—it gave me back pieces of myself I didn't know had gone missing. In every step, I was not only remembering her—I was finding me.

So here it is—our two Caminos. Hers, untouched and real. Mine, written with a mix of laughter, reverence, and the occasional meltdown. Both of us are carried by the same road.

INTRODUCTION
HER PATH BEFORE THE PATH

My Mum, Nuala Mary Brannigan, was born in Cork in 1944, the second child of Frank and Eileen, in the thin, ration-stamped air of wartime Ireland. Frank, a gentle man who spent his days at Ford Motors, was twenty-three years older than his sparkling young wife. And Eileen — well, she was all fire and brilliance, a mind built for bigger things than the narrow confines of 1930s Ireland ever allowed. She had scored nearly top in the country in Maths for her Leaving Cert — an extraordinary achievement, and utterly useless for a girl. No scholarships, no careers, just a polite pat on the head and the expectation she'd marry well. She was an immensely talented seamstress, gave the world's greatest hugs, and I loved her dearly. I wondered what she could have been if she had been born in a different time.

Mum grew up second in line among five siblings in a household that was as lively as it was loving. Somehow, she managed the remarkable feat of being everyone's favorite — her father's, her mother's (if her siblings are to be believed), and, more often than not, her siblings' as well. Even as life scattered them across Ireland and as far as Canada, she kept the threads tied, the one who made sure the family held together. She was the glue. A strong swimmer, a magnetic chatterbox, and an unrepentant flirt, she carried a kind of sparkle that drew people in and kept them close.

After secondary school, she left for Cardiff to study radiography. From there, Zurich called—not just because it sounded more glamorous, but because she'd always loved the idea of skiing. Never mind that she didn't speak a word of German. She simply bluffed her way through the application, certain that charm would cover any gaps. It did. The nurse who hired her was Andrea. Mum adored her, and when I came along, she gave me her name—a simple, beautiful inheritance.

When she returned to Cork, she took a trip to Galway with her then-boyfriend. Fate, being sneaky as ever, placed my father in her path that weekend. They met at the infamous Lydon's Bakery on Shop Street. They caught sight of each other across the room, stealing glances they pretended not to notice. He followed her back to her hotel, left a note at reception, and somehow that little gesture turned into a marriage, five children, and, eventually, a divorce. There was chaos and drama growing up with them, yes — but also love and adventure, and I have some great memories always to look back on.

Mum traded her profession for motherhood — a decision that, in truth, wasn't much of a decision at all back then. In her late thirties, Mum decided that she wanted her own pocket money for ski trips. So, alongside her best friend Regina, part ballerina, part comedienne, she co-founded Galway's first aerobics class. In a country where Irish housewives rarely had part-time jobs, and women certainly never took holidays on their own, this was radical stuff. Within weeks, the classes were packed with women who arrived weary and invisible, and left buzzing, gossiping, alive. Mum never quite realized the alchemy she'd created in that room: women reclaiming themselves for an hour. And yes, she got her ski trip. She got many. On the first trip, she left my father a note one morning: Gone skiing. Back in a week. Steel wrapped in spandex. Ahead of her time.

In her forties, Mum returned to radiography full-time, and I believe those were her happiest years. She thrived in her work, cherished being a mother, and still relished glamour—never one to dim her light. At fifty, when divorce came, she hurled herself into both work and travel, as if forward motion itself could shield her from the sting. Her passport became a testament to that momentum: Cambridge summer school, the slopes of Austria, weeks wandering through India, and, of course, the Camino de Santiago — the crown jewel of her adventures.

Looking back, I see now that the constant movement was more than wanderlust; it was her way of postponing the harder work of healing. Mum was never one for self-reflection. She preferred the outward gaze — the next plan, the next trip, the next adventure. Those journeys were not only quests for excitement but also escapes — not from her children, but from the shadows of her own past, the ghosts she rarely named. Yet what endures is not the darkness she fled, but the light she found along the way: freedom, laughter, herself. Stubborn to the last, she was slow to admit when she was the problem — when, indeed, she was. And knowing what I know now about the weight of unprocessed stress and the toll of buried pain, I can't help but wonder if that lifelong refusal to look inward helped pave the road for Alzheimer's, the disease quietly building its claim long before we gave it a name.

Mum adored being a mother and often joked that if my sister hadn't finally insisted she stop at five, she'd have happily kept going to ten. And truthfully, she was a different kind of mother to each of us—though I suspect that's the confession of every child in a large family, shaped as much by birth order and temperament as by the shifting seasons of a parent's life. What never wavered was her spirit: she was full of life, adventure, energy, and love. Glamorous and charming, affectionate and razor-witted, she could light up any room—or scorch it. Stubborn, fiery, and quick to go from zero to one hundred, she was an Irish woman through and through: passionate, feisty, and gloriously untamed.

At seventy-five, Alzheimer's arrived with cruel stealth. Officially, my sister Barbara received the diagnosis then, though the signs had crept in years before. We blamed chemo and radiation from her breast cancer at seventy for her forgetfulness and her quicksilver moods. But the truth revealed itself slowly and relentlessly.

Barbara, my angel-sister, became the architect of Mum's care. She managed everything: appointments, live-in help during Covid, converting her own basement into an apartment, and, finally, guiding Mum gently into full-time care. Five children in the family, but Barbara shouldered most of it. I carry an enormous weight of guilt and an even greater weight of gratitude for that. The toll on her was immense: her health, her energy, her own life put on hold, yet she never complained. I shudder to think what those years would have been like for Mum without her.

My brothers—Frank, Adrian, and Ben—each showed up

in their own way, shaped by their lives, their limits, and their love. It was hard then, and it's still hard now. We've each carried Mum's loss differently, but I know they're there if I need them.

Living far away gave me an easy excuse and a difficult ache. I flew home two or three times a year, trying to cover days so Barbara could rest, taking Mum on little trips, and arranging escapes for my sister. But it was never enough. It never could be. Distance both shields you and breaks you.

Maybe my gift was to make sure her footsteps weren't lost to time—that her Camino, her bravado, her laughter would live on in the telling, urging others toward the freedom she found on the road.

CHAPTER 1

DEPARTURE LOUNGE FOR THE SOUL

August 28th – San Diego to London Heathrow

Backpack strapped tight. For the first time in 15 years of corporate travel, I'm not sprinting toward a terminal Starbucks, waving my platinum status like a badge of self-worth, or expensing a nonfat latte with a side of existential dread. I'm just… walking. Through the airport. No blazer. No laptop bag. No PowerPoint slides that require some final finessing, just in case Wi-Fi is again inoperable in flight: just me, a backpack, and the terrifying luxury of having no idea what comes next.

The last time I wore a backpack like this was 1999, on my way to Thailand with my then-boyfriend, now husband, Neil and a dog-eared Lonely Planet. That girl thought she was fearless. Today, I feel like her again: wide-eyed, slightly underpacked, and about to learn that 15 pounds of "essentials" feels like a small boulder when you're lugging it across airports.

And yet, I'm smiling. One of those rare, involuntary grins

that starts somewhere in your gut and hijacks your whole face. My heart? A cocktail of joy and guilt.

Six weeks. That's how long I'll be walking the Camino de Santiago. Six weeks of my life that feel both selfish and essential.

It's also pretty close to the exact number of nights I've jolted awake at 3 a.m. with my brain whispering, "You're leaving Neil and Ryan for how long again?"

But they'll be fine. Better than fine. There will be frozen pizzas, mismatched laundry, and possibly a few moments when they miss me enough to clean the kitchen before I come home. My 14-year-old might even secretly enjoy the space because, lately, quite honestly and by his own direct admission, I've been around just a little too much... which leads me to my career departure.

Technically, I left my job.

But like all great corporate breakups, it was "complicated." Political. A sudden executive departure triggered the usual reorg and land grab—and I landed on the wrong side of it. Looking back, I can own the fact that I didn't see it coming soon enough or move myself into a stronger position. In my heart of hearts, I never believed it would play out that way.

I had loved the company and my team. After being a year-over-year top performer, I assumed that alone would guarantee a role aligned with my capabilities and experience. The truth is, while you're told, "it's not personal," it feels incredibly personal. I had hoped the leadership team would step in with the reorganization and offer me something compelling worth staying for. What they offered, they knew I wouldn't accept. That was the point. And that's what hurt. I'm also aware that at senior levels, there are fewer rungs on the ladder, and the ones above are often already full. It can feel like that final leg of Everest: increasingly crowded, precarious, and unforgiving. Some people make it to the summit; others fall off or turn back. So, I turned back.

I didn't confront anyone or call anyone out. I didn't demand answers or wage a battle I knew I'd already lost. Like every good marketer, I controlled the narrative. I chose the high road because I've always believed there's a kind of grace in a quiet, dignified exit.

Do I wish people would have stepped up for me—championed me the way I had championed them? Of course. But in my heart, I knew it was time to go. It was time for another adventure and for leadership that believed in me as much as I believed in myself.

Even harder to admit—but while I'm pouring my heart out here—is that I think I had no fight left in me. I was hurt, depleted, and when people stop believing in you, it's dangerously easy to stop believing in yourself. Between my mother's illness, the upheaval of menopause reshaping my very chemistry, and the deep, gnawing disappointment of it all, I was exhausted—not the kind of tired that sleep could cure, but a soul-level fatigue.

So I left. Not in anger, but with a kind of bittersweet clarity. Maybe it was part courage, part surrender, but it was mine. A quiet exit, my version of closing the door with my head held high, ready to face whatever life—and the Camino—had to teach me next.

The Camino was, in many ways, everything the corporate world wasn't. Raw. Real. Un-curated. Out there, it wouldn't matter who I was or what I'd achieved, just whether I could keep putting one foot in front of the other.

Packing for the Camino was a cross between a military operation and an exorcism. I'd read that a pilgrim's pack should weigh no more than 10% of your body weight, which is apparently the universal code for "throw out 80% of your stuff and pray you don't regret it."

What I Thought I Needed:

Hair straightener (because frizz is the enemy of confidence).

Full skincare routine: cleanser, serum, moisturizer.

Three shades of blush. (I'm a blush addict; this is my truth.)

Perfume, because maybe I'd run into Javier Bardem?

A book because I thought I'd have the energy to read after 30 km of walking. (Ha.)

What I Actually Packed:

2 merino wool T-shirts (fast-drying, allegedly smell-proof — "allegedly" doing heavy lifting there.)

2 pairs of shorts.

1 pair of leggings for cooler days.

3 pairs of underwear (rotate, wash, repeat).

3 pairs of socks, including the life-saving toe socks that prevent blisters.

1 poncho.

A microfleece (which, spoiler alert, doubled as a pillow, emotional support blanket, and occasional tablecloth).

A travel towel so small it could be mistaken for a napkin.

Sandals (hideous but heavenly for tired feet).

A silk sleeping liner for protection in those questionable, bedbug-infested Albergue beds.

A hat that screamed "Dora the Explorer."

A refillable water bottle.

A headlamp that made me feel like a miner in the dark.

One sacred tube of mascara and lip gloss. (I am not a savage.)

The departure lounge was buzzing with the usual chaos—families juggling iPads and snacks, business travelers barking into headsets, and me, sitting cross-legged in the corner like some blissed-out dropout. I was just sitting, staring at my boarding pass and wondering what the hell I had signed up for.

And yet, as my flight was called, I felt that familiar pull—the one you get before a big adventure when fear and excitement braid themselves together into something almost electric.

TINY PILGRIM TRUTH:

Life is a lot like air travel—once you're in the air, there's no turning back. You're already on your way, ready or not.

CHAPTER 2

BRIGHTON TO BIARRITZ – A FAREWELL TO FANCY

Friday, August 30th

Gatwick Airport. My Camino countdown had officially begun. I had just wrapped up a weekend of unapologetic indulgence in Brighton with my dear friend Andrew and his husband Mike—the kind of hosts who could run a masterclass in hospitality, dog devotion, and spontaneous show tunes. Think Michelin-star generosity meets Broadway's greatest hits, all served with a smooth bottle of Bordeaux and a side of mischief.

Brighton, England's rebellious, eccentric seaside darling, blew me away. How had this place never been on my radar? We wandered through its candy-colored lanes, past shops selling everything from vintage vinyl records to artisan coffee, and dined (entirely out of character for my soon-to-be pilgrim aesthetic) at both "The Ivy" and the gloriously chic "Rockwater" restaurants. There I was, dressed like a misplaced yoga instructor who had taken a wrong turn on the way to a silent retreat.

Andrew and I met at Qualcomm, and from the first conversation, I knew—or maybe just desperately hoped—that we'd be friends. He's one of those rare people who can wear a thousand hats, all of them essential: confidant, mentor, co-conspirator, and, if we're honest, family. Aren't friends really just the family we get to choose?

He was brilliant—the kind of smart that lights up a room —but also wickedly funny, occasionally absurd, and always, always 100% real. No masks, no games. Just honesty, wit, and the kind of loyalty that's hard to come by in corporate hallways. His friendship wasn't just a highlight of my Qualcomm years; it was one of the great gifts of that entire chapter of my life.

Boston, their colossal, incredibly spoiled-yet-charming Weimaraner, fell head over paws for me. By night two, he'd claimed a spot in my bed. Given that he'd be the last male to share it for the next 45 days, I figured I'd take what I could get—fur, drool, and all.

Truth be told, I was spoiled too. And I knew my days of spoiling were numbered. But not quite yet. Ahead lay one more evening of decadence—in Biarritz, that French beauty queen of the Atlantic, with her old-world glamour, sun-kissed promenades, and a kind of romance that whispers of emperors, artists, and scandalous summer love. I could have landed and gone straight to the starting point of Roncesvalles, but I decided to indulge myself with a little "South of France" sightseeing before I assumed pilgrim status. I could have landed and marched straight to Roncesvalles, all business, boots laced, halo polished. But instead, I gave myself permission to linger — a little "South of France" detour, a last sip of indulgence before trading it all for the blisters, dust, and humility of the Camino.

I landed at 10 p.m., stepping into air that was equal parts warm and sultry, like the exhale of a place that knows it doesn't have to try too hard. France always strikes me as charmingly chaotic—grace and disorder perfectly coexisting—and I was thrilled to find that Biarritz, even late at night, still hummed with energy. Cafés and restaurants spilled onto the pavements, their tables buzzing with conversations and wine glasses clinking, as if the entire town collectively agreed that evenings were made for lingering, not rushing home.

The Hôtel Cosmopolitain, my crash pad for the night, was a stunner—a petite Parisian cousin of New York's Flatiron, all angles and attitude. I tossed my weary backpack (bulging at the seams) onto the floor and went in search of food. A few blocks away, at "Prima les Colonnes," I found what can only be described as divine intervention: the best pizza I have ever eaten. Thin, blistered crust; molten, salty cheese; and yes, I still had room for dessert. I took it as a sign from the Camino gods that I was on the right path—at least gastronomically.

Afterward, I strolled down to La Grande Plage, which, in classic French understatement, translates simply to "The Big Beach." It was vast, romantic, and vibrating with late-summer energy. Couples kissed like they'd invented kissing. Teenagers dared each other into the surf, shrieking with laughter. And dogs roamed leashless and free, as if they too had thrown off the invisible rules of modern life.

I wandered up to the grand Hôtel du Palais, the seaside palace Napoleon III built for his Empress Eugénie. My sister had brought Mum here for her 60th birthday back in 2005, and she'd adored it. Mum adored anything to do with

Napoleon—ancestors included. She owned nearly every book ever written about him, and while his accomplishments were undeniable, I never quite understood her devotion, which verged on obsession. To be fair, her loyalties were split — Napoleon shared shelf space with Michael Collins, whom she worshipped with equal ferocity.

Mum was a voracious reader, but not a wide one; once she fixated on a subject, she devoured it whole. I, in complete contrast, was the consummate generalist. Everything and anything interested me. I wondered now, with her Alzheimer's, did she miss those books? Where did her mind travel when she no longer had pages to disappear into?

Standing there, outside the Empress's old villa, I made a quiet promise to myself: tomorrow I'd return for my own imperial moment.

By 11:30 p.m., I was back at the hotel, bent over the sink, scrubbing underwear. Biarritz had given me beaches, boulevards, and a palace fit for an empress — and here I was sudsing my knickers like a scullery maid. Glamorous? Hardly. But as it turned out, these small, unflattering rituals would become the quiet heartbeat of the journey.

THE GLAMOROUS TRUTH

Palaces are optional. Clean underwear is not.

CHAPTER 3

"GOODBYE GOURMET, HELLO GRANOLA BARS"

August 31st – Biarritz and Bayonne

I let myself sleep in, trusting my internal compass over alarm clocks. The Hôtel Cosmopolitain's Gatsby-esque café rewarded me with a latte and a still-warm pastry, and for a brief, glorious moment, I sat there pretending to be a French intellectual. I almost pulled it off until I tipped foamed milk across my guidebook—so much for "je ne sais quoi."

I decided to head out without a map, armed only with curiosity and the kind of blind confidence that says, "How lost can I really get in a beach town?" There's something liberating about not having a plan—just letting the streets, the breeze, and the sound of the waves tell you where to go.

The Grand Plage was in full summer glamour; its candy-striped umbrellas flung across the sand like vintage postcards. Against the cerulean sky, it all looked almost too perfect, like a film set waiting for Catherine Deneuve to stroll through in a wide-brimmed hat. At the far end of the beach, the lighthouse stood like a patient sentinel. So, I followed it, wandering the cliffside path—a mix of fairy-tale charm and calf-burning fitness test. At the top, a tiny café served espresso so good it felt like a cinematic moment, the kind where violins swell, and you suddenly think life has more meaning just because you're holding a porcelain cup.

After lunch, I ambled back to the beach. I remembered Mum's sage advice: "Travel like a local, not a tourist." So I stopped, stripped down, and took a swim, followed by a sunbathing session that lasted just long enough to feel like I'd earned my place on the sand. Locals lounged effortlessly, perfectly tanned and armed with little more than sunscreen, a towel, and a hat. There was something so beautiful in that simplicity. The beach, the ocean, the sun. It was enough. Americans, on the other hand, treat beach days like a moon landing—coolers, umbrellas, collapsible carts, enough snacks to survive a famine, and five SPF variations, just in case.

Here, even bikini tops seemed optional. I admired their confidence and their cheekbones—all four of them.

Later, in what can only be described as a small miracle of fake-it-till-you-make-it confidence, I managed to glide past the Hôtel du Palais guard simply by announcing I was "meeting a guest for coffee." I wasn't. But I knew Mum would've cheered me on from the sidelines. She loved this place, its history, and its unapologetic grandeur. As I mentioned, she adored all things Napoleon—every generation of him. Her taste in heroes was nothing if not eclectic: Michael Collins, Nehru, Meatloaf, and really any man over sixty with a full head of hair, quick wit, and a voice you could happily let narrate your life.

By mid-afternoon, I wandered through Les Halles de Biarritz, the town's famed food market. It was the kind of sensory overload that makes you briefly consider moving to France just to live off figs and cheese. I feasted on Bayonne ham, a sinful slice of gâteau Basque, and a glass of Châteauneuf-du-Pape that made me consider relocating instantly to this charming small town.

Charming it was, but my destination it was not. I reluctantly collected my things, grabbed a taxi, and headed for Bayonne—my final stop before the Camino would officially begin. The ride felt like the quiet breath before a leap, the last soft edge of comfort before the path would strip me down to the essentials. Bayonne awaited like a prologue in stone and history, whispering, 'Tomorrow, the real story begins.'

TINY PILGRIM TRUTH:

The old world still knows the secret — wine, bread, sea air. Everything else is just decoration.

CHAPTER 4

THE CALM BEFORE THE CAMINO

Sunday, September 1 – Bayonne to St. Jean Pied de Port

After a luxurious four hours of sleep, though, whether the culprit was menopause or pre-pilgrimage nerves, I was unsure. But I woke looking like someone who had already completed all 35 days of the Camino and was ready for a nap, not a noble quest.

Still, I peeled myself out of bed and onto the cobbled lanes of Bayonne, the streets hushed and glistening in that soft, cinematic way early morning light hits medieval stone. It felt like I'd rented the town for a private farewell—it was so quiet and peaceful.

The train to St. Jean Pied de Port was a short stroll across the sleepy city, and by 7:45, I found myself in a carriage that felt strangely deserted, with just three other backpackers scattered in all corners of the carriage. For a moment, I wondered if I'd misread the schedule or taken a wrong turn. Shouldn't more people be heading toward this world-renowned pilgrimage? This was the main departure point to St. Jean Pied-de-

Port, with only three trains running each day. Naturally, I found myself on the very first, no surprise to anyone who knows me. That early-riser instinct became a quiet tradition, one that carried me all along the Camino.

As the train hummed forward, the Basque countryside unfolded in glorious green waves: rolling hills flecked with the architectural equivalent of an Instagram filter—white-washed farmhouses with blood-red roofs and sage-green shutters. Sheep grazed like extras in a period film.

Roughly ninety minutes later, we slid into St. Jean Pied de Port, a name that sounds poetic in French and slightly stern in English ("Foot of the Pass," if you're wondering). Nestled in the Pyrenees like a jewel in a velvet box, St. Jean is the official starting point of the Camino Francés, the most famous of the pilgrimage routes to Santiago de Compostela. It has welcomed wanderers for over a millennium, ever since King Alfonso II of Asturias first walked westward to honor the newly discovered remains of St. James around the year 820. Since then, millions of monks, soldiers, and sinners, seekers have followed in his footsteps, each hoping to lose something, find something, or simply walk off the weight of the world.

When I arrived just after 10 a.m., the town was stretching awake. Despite already inhaling a coffee and croissant in Bayonne (which would become my monotonous morning ritual for the next six weeks), I was ready for round two plus a slice of the local Gateaux Basque, a butter-forward cake with a personality as rich as its filling. Honestly, it's a small miracle the Camino doesn't come with a weight-gain warning label. I consoled myself with the fact that I'd be walking 850 kilometers. Surely that neutralizes at least some of the calories, right?

After finding my hotel, the Hotel-Restaurant des Remparts, which charmingly doubles as a launch pad for nervous pilgrims, I explored the town, climbing the ramparts that still circle the old village like a medieval embrace. The views stretched all the way to the mountains I'd be foolishly climbing tomorrow. I stuffed half a jambon-fromage baguette into my pack and the other half into my face (multitasking!) and marveled that, so far, pilgrim cuisine was hardly penitential.

Unlike my mother, who, at 68, set out with no bookings and no apps, I had reserved my first four nights of lodging. I told myself it was smart. Practical. Slightly Type A. But mostly, it was kindness to my future self. In my Type A defense, the Camino has seen a surge in walkers ever since the 2010 film *The Way* with Martin Sheen turned it into a mainstream pilgrimage. In 2012, around 192,000 pilgrims completed the journey; by 2024, that number had soared past 440,000. Mum went full Camino-cowgirl, rolling into towns and charming her way into beds like a silver-haired Mary on a donkey (minus the donkey, plus an Osprey backpack). I, on the other hand, had apps. Glorious, stress-reducing apps. Call it planned spontaneity. If that's not already a term, it should be. At the pilgrim office, I received my "credencial" (Camino passport) and the traditional scallop shell, which I proudly tied to my backpack. It clinked reassuringly as I walked, like a tiny bell that whispered, "You're doing this thing."

Inside the Church of Notre Dame, I lit three candles. One for my granny, because since she passed in 1995, I've made it a habit to light a candle in every Catholic church I enter, out of love and superstition in equal measure. One for my mother, because this entire journey is for her. And one for me, because if I'm walking 500 miles across Spain, I'd like a little divine backup.

Later, with a cold beer in hand and the Basque sun beginning to soften, I sat and considered my why. Why was I here, really? What was I hoping to find? And then, gently and without drama, the answer came: to follow the breadcrumbs my mother left behind, to piece together the parts of her I maybe never truly knew, and to inhabit, at least for a while, a place of joy that belonged entirely to me. Piece of cake, I smiled to myself.

By 10 p.m., the lights were out. My pack was ready. My clothes were drying. And my body—God bless it—was beginning to understand that tomorrow, the real journey begins. Not just across Spain, but inward.

TINY PILGRIM TRUTH:

Every pilgrimage begins twice—once when you pack your bag and again when you finally understand why you're carrying it.

CHAPTER 5

FEET ON THE GROUND, HEAD IN THE CLOUDS

September 2 – Day 1: St. Jean Pied de Port to Roncesvalles (25.1 km)

I woke to a silence that felt almost sacred, pre-dawn and heavy with anticipation. My room was dim, my breath steady, my thoughts anything but. My first ritual of Transcendental Meditation grounded me, though it felt more like a whispered plea than a mantra. The mountains waited outside, silhouetted by a sky not yet committed to day.

There's magic in beginnings, especially those that ask everything of you.

My mother always said, "Start how you mean to go on." So I began not with fanfare, but with reverence. With a croissant, a strong and large cup of coffee, and the feeling that my feet were about to remember something my head hadn't yet learned.

Six thousand miles from home, I feel strangely rooted. My family, my mum, and my friends may be scattered across time zones, but I carry their voices and spirit with me: every encouragement, every laugh, every warning to "pack lighter." At the invisible starting line, I am alone but not lonely.

Outside, the world was breathtaking. St. Jean still slept under a thin veil of dawn, and the path ahead pointed up—impossibly, unapologetically up, up through the Napoléon Route.

It's the most famous and feared start to the Camino Francés. Originally carved into history by Roman legions, then marched by Napoleon's troops in 1808 on their doomed way into Spain (it hadn't gone well for them, and I hoped it would go better for me). The route today challenges pilgrims with 1,400 meters of steep ascent over the Pyrenees. They don't tell you that when you pick up your pilgrim passport. They just smile and hand you a scallop shell.

As I climbed, each step whispered, "Here we go." The fog clung to the ridges like a secret, and the landscape unfolded with a kind of mythic patience, with lush meadows, wind-shaped trees, and sheep scattered across the hills. Sheep lounged like zen masters on the hillside, and wild horses stood like sentinels in the mist. As I climbed higher, the clouds floated below as if I'd climbed into the sky. The air was so pure it felt like it belonged to another century.

Around midmorning, I found rhythm with Elena, a solo walker from Florence. It was her second Camino. We didn't talk much; we didn't need to. Her presence felt like a page I didn't need to turn yet.

I passed Bruce and Louise, a sweet, still, admirably besotted elderly couple from the UK, walking at their own slower, sweeter pace. We traded smiles and blisters in progress, then parted with a warm "Buen Camino." No small talk required. No expectation to linger. Just kindness in motion.

The rain, which had been forecast, must have decided we pilgrims had enough on our plates. Instead, we walked through clouds that hovered beneath us, turning the mountain into something out of a dream where the heroine has slightly swollen ankles.

And then, after hours of climbing and floating and wondering if my thighs would file for divorce, I began the descent into Roncesvalles.

It was like entering a story carved out of time—tiny, beautiful, and timelessly medieval.

Roncesvalles—or "Valley of Thorns" has echoed with history for over a millennium. It's here that Charlemagne's army suffered a bloody defeat in 778, an ambush immortalized in The Song of Roland, one of the oldest surviving works of French literature. Pilgrims have been passing through ever since with soldiers, sinners, saints, and now… me, with my aching legs and half-crushed protein bar.

The monastery loomed through the mist, a stone fortress of faith and history. It looked exactly like the kind of place where someone might receive a vision or at least a really strong cup of tea.

I had splurged on a private room at the adjoining hotel, a Camino luxury I didn't even bother to justify. In Roncesvalles, it was either this or the monastery hostel. Later, I heard the hostel had filled by midafternoon, leaving late-arriving pilgrims to trudge on to the next town in the dark. In that moment, my forward-thinking self felt like a genius.

In the lobby, a flyer for a €30 massage caught my eye and, quite possibly, saved my soul. I booked it without hesitation. After all, it's best to take this pilgrimage transition slowly. An hour later, I emerged limber, grateful, and only slightly embarrassed at how completely reborn I felt.

Dinner was served in a warmly lit dining room with white tablecloths, flickering candles, and the gentle clink of cutlery, making it feel more like "Downton Abbey" than a dusty pilgrim dorm. From across the room, I struck up a conversation with a gentleman named Ornesto, a silver-haired Californian with the kind of easy laugh that suggested he'd survived a few plot twists. Within minutes, he waved me over to join him, chivalry clearly not dead in Santa Barbara.

He was taking a six-month sabbatical post-divorce, which he described with a mix of honesty, humor, and the unmistakable glow of someone who had just remembered what it felt like to put himself first. I liked him immediately.

After dinner, I drifted into the 13th-century church beside the monastery for the pilgrim's mass. Candles flickered in iron sconces. The pews creaked under the weight of dozens of stories, each cloaked in different languages and lives. When the priest offered the pilgrim's blessing, I not just heard it, but felt it, deep and wide and old.

I thought of Mum again. She walked this same path twelve years ago. Stood in this very church. Lit her own candle, carried her own longings. And now, here I was. Lighting one for her. Carrying them both.

My first day—a heavenly day—is over.

I'm grateful. Grateful to be here. Grateful to feel alive in every sense of the word.

TINY PILGRIM TRUTH:

If life ever hands you a chance—take it. Say yes. Explore the world. Explore yourself.

CHAPTER 6

OF WITCHES, RABIES, AND RAIN

September 3 – Day 2: Roncesvalles to Zubiri (25 km)

The Camino, like life, doesn't always respect your best-laid plans or your 5-minute snooze button.

I had every intention of rising before dawn and gliding out of Roncesvalles like a mystical morning pilgrim, aglow with purpose. Instead, I hit snooze once. Then again. Then... well, you know how that story ends. I justified the extra hour in bed as a spiritual choice, as surely slowing down was the whole point of this experience, right? Besides, the rain outside sounded like someone had unleashed a biblical flood. Maybe it would pass if I just meditated... horizontally.

Eventually, I emerged into the world, soggy and humbled, and headed to breakfast only to accidentally sit in the "cheap" breakfast slot. This was swiftly and awkwardly pointed out by a hotel staffer who herded me toward the upgraded seating mid-conversation with Adrian from the UK. Not my proudest egalitarian moment. I'd come to the Camino to escape class distinctions, not reenact them in a croissant line.

In the new, apparently posher breakfast zone, I grabbed an admittedly identical-looking but reclassified first-class croissant, a boiled egg, and a slice of questionable cheese. I struck up a conversation with Sonya from Dublin. Now, if you know Irish people, you know there are two kinds of Dubs: the fast-talking, story-spinning, heart-on-the-sleeve type, and the cool, slightly skeptical I'll chat, but don't get comfortable slow to get to know type. Sonya was definitely the latter. I trusted I could break through, and my optimism paid off. We had a good talk, and I could tell she was cut from strong cloth. By 8:30, I was finally on the road.

And what a road it was.

Lashing rain. Cold. September. Spain. Something didn't compute. I had clearly misunderstood the concept of "Mediterranean climate". With my poncho draped over me like an original pilgrim, I trudged out with the other water-logged pilgrims, most clanking along in trios or more, trekking poles tapping, massive packs swaying. I was glad to be on my own. That was the point of coming here: no waiting, no syncing to anyone else's rhythm. Just me, my pace, and the road. A free spirit for the first time in many, many years.

The forest was magical. A canopy of ancient trees arched overhead, whispering secrets through the drizzle. These woods, I had read earlier, were once home to the "sorginak"—women known as witches from the 13th to 16th centuries. Far from broomsticks and cauldrons, these women were midwives, herbalists, and community healers, basically the wellness influencers of medieval Navarre. They gathered herbs, mixed tinctures, held seasonal ceremonies, and yes, dared to exist with knowledge and autonomy. Naturally, the Inquisition couldn't have that. Hundreds were burned in nearby Burguete, their "gatherings" rebranded as "sabbats," their healing as "heresy."

Walking through those woods, it wasn't hard to imagine the echo of chants, the rustle of skirts, the scent of lavender and ash. It also wasn't hard to imagine myself among them: loud, independent, opinionated. I would've been toast in 14th-century Spain—burned before breakfast.

After an hour, I stopped for coffee, warmed my hands on the mug, and continued to Burguete, a town that still carries a slightly haunted air, even in daylight. The rain softened, and the walk was mostly gentle until the last 5 kilometers, which was all descent and pain. My knees staged a small protest.

I arrived in Zubiri around 3:30 p.m. and, in a classic Camino move, accidentally checked into the wrong hostel. In my defense, it shared a name, "Pensión Amets," with the correct one. Different places, same signage. Not ideal when your brain feels like it's been waterlogged and scrambled.

By then, my body was sore. I collapsed on the bed like a felled tree and woke up an hour later, mildly confused and still damp. After a shower, I ventured out for food and found myself at a lively little bar-café, full of pilgrims circled around an outdoor table deep into their second (or fourth?) glass of wine. The volume was high, the laughter infectious, and there were some familiar faces. But I wasn't in the mood for company.

Not yet.

I had set an intention to walk the first part of this journey solo. I didn't want to bond too early or get swept up in a pack. I needed space. For what, I was not quite sure. For grief, for thoughts, for whatever this pilgrimage was trying to teach me? I wasn't intentionally avoiding people; I was just intentionally not seeking them out. I would soon discover that the Camino has a perfect sense of timing. The right people, the right moments, they appear exactly when you need them.

For dinner, I grabbed a simple sandwich and sat by the river in front of Puente de la Rabia—the "Rabies Bridge." Legend says that animals led across it three times could be cured of rabies. Naturally, I wondered what it might cure me of. Heartache? Restlessness? Ambition? I walked across three times just to be sure. My knees hated me, but superstition won.

As I sat by the river, the loneliness crept in. Not overwhelming, just a soft ache. Where was this river going? Where was I going? I felt the weight of the days ahead and wondered if I'd been overly ambitious in not scheduling any rest days. My body clearly thought so.

Also, was I really the only person not using walking poles? And why were there so few solo walkers? Pairs were the order of the day—married couples, best friends, fathers and sons. Me? Just me.

But somehow, that felt right.

I headed to bed early, wondering what tomorrow would bring. I slept deeply, like the dead—or perhaps like a witch finally at rest, soothed by the knowledge that the fire, this time, had not come for her.

TINY PILGRIM TRUTH

Some days, the Camino tests your spirit with rain, legends, and the wrong hostel. But if you walk through the ache, across the doubt, and maybe over a medieval bridge three times for good luck, what you find isn't magic. It's resilience, disguised as your own two feet.

CHAPTER 7

COFFEE, KALIMOTXO, AND THE COMPANY WE KEEP

September 4 - Day 3: Zubiri to Pamplona (20.9km)

The day began with the kind of breakfast that makes you believe in human connection before your second cup of coffee. A mismatched crew gathered around the communal table at the pension: two Kiwi girls, Maggie and Audrey, bright-eyed and banana-obsessed; Ornesto, my Camino confidant from Roncesvalles; a charmingly bickering pair of British retirees, Amy and Sara with a suspicious number of tea bags; and Mike, the American who somehow managed to walk eight bonus miles yesterday by getting completely and utterly lost.

Now, getting lost on the Camino takes real talent. The route is marked with yellow arrows, scallop shells, and, in some towns, actual brass markers in the pavement. Not to mention the nearly always sight of some fellow pilgrim in front or behind you, unless, like me, you leave before sunrise to avoid. But Mike? Head down, eyes glued to his Camino GPS app was blissfully unaware of the very real world around him. Isn't the whole point of this ancient pilgrimage to disconnect? To stop scrolling, start walking, and maybe find yourself somewhere between here and Santiago?

Ornesto and I walked together that day, through intermittent drizzle that left us damp but not miserable. He told me he was recently divorced, traveling for three months across Europe to reset his life compass. His two grown kids supported his adventure. So did his three suitcases, one of which, he confessed, was packed entirely with protein bars and electrolyte packets. I teased him relentlessly. He took it well. "Camino" baggage, both literal and metaphorical, gets lighter the longer you walk. And talk.

He was shipping his bags ahead with the help of the very handy pilgrim transport service. Later on the Camino, I did this—just once. I felt like I was cheating on my backpack and myself. I missed its weight, its presence—like some loyal, lumpy friend strapped to my spine. I never did it again.

We didn't stop much, except for one glorious caffeine-fueled break two kilometers outside Pamplona. Two lattes and a tortada later, I felt reborn. Sugar, caffeine, and scenery —heaven.

We arrived at the ancient walls of Pamplona, said our goodbyes, and went separate ways into the city. That's the Camino for you: intense friendships born in hours and dissolved in minutes with a hug and a wave. In tiny villages, pilgrims are everywhere. In big cities like Pamplona, you can walk for blocks without spotting a single scallop shell.

Pamplona—most famously known for its heart-pounding Running of the Bulls— is much more than that singular act of chaos. Founded by the Romans in 75 BC and once a strategic fortress city, its winding cobblestone streets and thick medieval walls echo with the footsteps of centuries. At one point, Pamplona was the capital of the Kingdom of Navarre. It has survived sieges, civil wars, and Hemingway's bar tab.

I wandered through the city to my hotel, an extra 2km out the other side, dropped my pack, then turned around and did it all again for dinner in the city center. But I had a date, with myself at Café Iruña, Hemingway's haunt in the iconic Plaza del Castillo. Founded in 1888, it was the first building in Pamplona lit by electricity, a detail that somehow made my glass of kalimotxo (red wine and Coca-Cola, a local favourite) feel both timeless and rebelliously modern.

As I sat there, surrounded by chatter and clinking glasses, I found myself lost not in my phone, but in thought. How many conversations, tears, seductions, and declarations happened within these walls? How many people passed through, thinking their story was the centre of the universe?

We all do it. We think our lives are epic sagas when really, we're footnotes. And that's oddly comforting. The only thing that truly matters is how we lived, who we loved, what kindness we offered, and what remains in the hearts of those we touched.

Today, I hoped I had touched a life.

Ivan, 85, from Australia, was inching his way through Pamplona when I caught up. I asked if I could walk with him. His daughters called him daily, worried sick. He had trained for months to be here, determined to do at least part of the Camino. We talked, we laughed, we shared the road for a while. Before I left, I told him, very truthfully, that I was in awe of him.

I was 50. Mum had been 68. Ivan was 85. Turns out the Camino doesn't have an age limit. Just a heartbeat and a will.

TINY PILGRIM TRUTH

The Camino gives you strangers who feel like old friends, conversations that carry more than your pack ever could, and the quiet grace of realizing that letting go and holding on can happen in the same step.

CHAPTER 8

WHEN DINNER COMES WITH A LESSON

Sept 5 - Day 4: Pamplona to Puente La Reina (23.8 km)

I shared breakfast at the pension with Maggie and Gary, a charming, retired couple from LA. It was a cool, rain-free morning, which was always worth a silent thank-you to the Camino gods.

I was ready to leave Pamplona, but Pamplona was apparently not ready to let go of me. Locating the Camino markers was a navigational exercise in patience. The Camino blue arrows were hard to find, and my GPS was questionable. Big cities are full of distractions and detours, and it took me a few second-guesses before I'd cleared the suburbs. But once I did, the rhythm returned. Open countryside, golden fields, and the familiar soundtrack of footsteps and distant chatter. A steady climb through Zariquiegui and up to Alto de Perdón delivered the payoff: sweeping views, vineyards in every direction, and the distant Pyrenees shrinking behind me. One hundred kilometers down. Quiet pride took up residence in my chest.

The trail was lively but never crowded. I passed and was

passed, and always had enough solitude to think. The smell in the countryside was so beautiful, alive, earthy and fresh. It made me think of Mum.

She always smelled wonderful. The kind of person you smelled before you even saw her, though she was rarely quiet enough to sneak up on anyone. Her scent was singular, unwavering: Coco Chanel. I still spritz it into the air at department stores just to feel her near. It lingers differently on me, but for that brief second, suspended in air, it's her. It makes me smile, or my eyes well up. Sometimes both. Every time.

Tonight's Albergue was a private room, basic, clean, mine. After doing laundry (a deeply underrated Camino thrill), I took myself to Bidean, a small restaurant the manager had recommended. The pizza was next-level, and I paired it with two unapologetic glasses of red wine. The Camino makes indulgence feel entirely justified. You walk. You earn.

Over dinner, reading my Camino book entry for the day, I stumbled upon a question that stopped me in my tracks. Am I balancing the busyness of my ego with the being-ness of my spirit? A Camino-sized question, worthy of the miles. I wondered, am I letting my ego's constant striving, proving, and busyness drown out the quiet presence of my true self—my spirit? I began to see that the ego and the spirit weren't enemies. The ego laced my boots each morning; the spirit noticed the sunrise. The ego counted the kilometers; the spirit reminded me that the distance didn't matter. Out here, they learned to walk together, one pushing me forward, the other teaching me how to arrive.

Afterwards, I strolled to the Puente la Reina, the "Queen's Bridge." A striking 11th-century structure built for pilgrims like me to safely cross the river on their way west. It's elegant, enduring, and still standing strong after nearly a thousand years. That kind of quiet permanence stops you in your tracks—things that were built to last.

On my way back, I bumped into Elena from Day 1. She invited me to join her and a few others for dinner. I almost did, but my body and my spirit leaned toward solitude. I took her number and promised to reconnect. The Camino teaches you to tune in, to honor what you need, not just what's offered.

Back at the restaurant earlier, a woman named Assumpta from Seattle asked if she could join me. I paused. I had been looking forward to dining alone, but I said yes.

She shared that she was walking the Camino solo. She and her husband had planned to do it together, but he passed away two years ago. Now, she was walking for both of them.

When I went to pay, the waiter told me she already had.

In that quiet act, she honored her husband, included me in her ritual of remembrance, and reminded me that kindness isn't random here, it's the currency of the road. I promised myself I would pay it forward.

TINY PILGRIM TRUTH

Make room. Even when you think you don't want company, someone else might need yours. And sometimes, their story teaches you that the wisdom you've been searching for often arrives through someone else's words.

CHAPTER 9

RAIN, REROUTES, AND REVELATIONS

September 6 – Day 5: Puente la Reina to Estella (21.9 km)

I risk sounding like a broken record or a weathered travel cliché, but this was, without question, one of my favorite days on the Camino. And that's saying something because it began with all the promise of a root canal.

I had four hours of sleep, max, courtesy of a group of very on-brand Irish lads beneath my hostel balcony conducting a full-volume, no-intermission pub session until 3:30 a.m. Not exactly the sacred stillness I'd envisioned. With a 7:00 a.m. wake-up call looming, I briefly considered dedicating the rest of my pilgrimage to the prayer that these lads were not walking beyond this town.

If the sleep deprivation didn't set the tone, the weather did. Five minutes into the day, we had a monsoon—sheets of it, soaking every inch of dignity. Two out of my last five walking days have been rain-drenched. I began to wonder if Spain had quietly sold its soul to the west coast of Ireland.

But it's funny how quickly "disaster" softens into "just

part of the journey" when you've got decent rain gear and a willingness to laugh at yourself. Wrapped in a poncho and my trusty Tevas—fondly, and Camino-appropriately, dubbed my "Jesus sandals"—I carried on, soggy but oddly content.

Along the way, I met pilgrims. Some for a moment, others for a mile, and one, a German man named Jen Uwe, for an accidental detour. We shared exactly four words of common language between us, and yet somehow, through theatrical hand gestures and international optimism, we kept pace.

Until, of course, we didn't. Roughly two kilometers later, we realized we were gloriously, indisputably lost. The absence of backpacks and yellow arrows was a clue, but the empty road stretching into oblivion really drove it home. Thankfully, we spotted the town of Estella down in the valley in the distance—Estella the Beautiful, as it was known in the fifteenth century—and took a right at the next divine intervention.

After sharing a snack at a centuries-old abbey (cookies from him, chocolate from me, a fair cultural exchange), we found our way back to the Camino. Soon after, I bumped into Alistair from the UK and his two teenage sons, Charlie and Aonghus. Both proud half-marathoners, the boys were slightly mortified that their bags were being transported by van while silver-haired pilgrims marched past carrying their own. They repeatedly reminded me it was their dad's decision. Ah, adolescent pride—it's as heavy as any rucksack.

By evening, I arrived at the hostel to discover I'd be sharing a room with four others, and horror of horrors, I'd drawn the bottom bunk. A special kind of claustrophobia kicked in. I delayed my reckoning with it by fleeing to town and pouring a glass of wine on it.

Estella, however, more than made up for it. The town, with its winding streets, grand stone houses, regal palaces, convents, and churches at every turn, looked like a Caravaggio painting that had learned to flirt. I was utterly smitten.

On a whim, and in desperate need of dignity, I ducked into a tiny salon offering a €15 wash and blow-dry. It had been five days. No judgment. Emerging with a bouncy, clean mane and a soul that felt slightly restored, I sent a message to my accidental companions from the day: "Dinner?"

Jen, Uwe, and Alistair responded as if I'd invited them to Christmas. We met at Mondo, an unexpectedly chic Asian spot nestled between two churches and what may have been a centuries-old bakery. Over noodles and laughter, and later over Rioja at a wine-barrel table in the street, we talked, swapped stories, and stood in the shadow of history. It was one of those golden, cinematic evenings, the kind that feels both entirely of this world and not.

I wandered back to the hostel, full in both body and soul. I settled into what I had reframed in my mind as a cozy bottom bunk, hopeful that a few glasses of wine would hurry sleep along. The landlady had given us a code for the combination lock so we could slip back in at night, and I thought nothing more of it.

An hour later, I woke with my bladder issuing its end-of-day ultimatum, and panic hit. I realized I had absolutely no idea what the code was. If I left the room, I risked being locked out. Cue a claustrophobia-induced spiral: me whisper-arguing with myself in the dark.

Finally, in a stroke of unremarkable genius, I did what any rational adult would have done an hour earlier: I stuck my shoe in the door. Yes, a literal shoe. The same wine that had so kindly put me to sleep had clearly done nothing for my problem-solving skills.

TINY PILGRIM TRUTH:

We spend so much energy debating people who speak the same language—ideologically, politically, socially. What if we approached all our interactions with the same spirit as those who speak different languages—with curiosity, patience, and maybe a little less ego?

The world might not agree more, but it just might understand each other better.

CHAPTER 10

WHERE WINE FLOWS FREELY AND SO DO THOUGHTS

September 7– Day 5: Estella to Los Arcos (21.5 km)

I got a later start than usual this morning. Blame the seductive charms of Estella. One last slow wander through its cobbled lanes, grand stone archways, and early-bird cafés felt necessary. I thought I might be sad to leave such a beautiful town so soon, but the Camino was already teaching me the art of goodbye. It wasn't really leaving at all, just carrying the place with me, step by step, down the road.

I stopped at the legendary Fuente del Vino, the Wine Fountain, at the monastery of Irache. Installed by the local winery Bodegas Irache, it offers two taps: one for water and one for red wine. Pilgrims drink from it in reverence, amusement, or confusion—often all three.

There's an inscription beside it: "Peregrino, si quieres llegar a Santiago con fuerza y vitalidad, de este gran vino toma un sorbo y brinda por la felicidad." ("Pilgrim, if you wish to reach Santiago with strength and vitality, take a sip of this great wine and toast to happiness.")

I did just that: cupped hand, one mouthful. Cold. Sacred. Slightly tannic. Perfect.

And in that moment, I wasn't thinking about mileage, or my feet, or dinner. I was thinking about thirst. Not for wine. For joy. For clarity. For breathing room. I don't yet know how to fully quench that kind of thirst. But out here, step by step, breath by breath, story by story, I am filling my cup, and it tastes like more.

The trail out was all-natural terrain, winding through stoic oak-lined hills toward Villamayor de Monjardin, a village that could never take a bad photo. I stopped for a coffee at the local café with a view included. Just as I was singing the praises of Spanish coffee with Sonya from Dublin, whom I had just bumped into, and lifted the cup for a celebratory sip, a large fly bobbed up like it owned the place. We burst out laughing and laughed until our coffee went cold. Sometimes the smallest interruptions land with perfect comic timing.

The sun reasserted itself after a few wet, rather melancholic days, and the heat felt less like punishment and more like a return to form. Dry socks, dry spirits. It really is the little things.

I arrived in Los Arcos around 3:00 PM, checking into the delightfully simple Pensión Mavi. For those unfamiliar, a pensión in Spain is a family-run guesthouse, usually somewhere between a hostel and a hotel in spirit and price. Often charming, sometimes eccentric, always human. Much like the Camino itself.

Los Arcos is a town of roughly 1,200 souls, a place where time has learned to walk slowly. Once a crucial stop on the medieval Camino, it thrived as a crossroads for pilgrims, traders, and the occasional knight with a sore back. Today, it retains a dignified humility, a long, sunbaked plaza ringed with cafés, the clink of wine glasses echoing off stone walls, and the occasional church bell slicing through the breeze like a reminder to look up.

After the obligatory siesta (when in Spain...), I joined the lively square scene where pilgrims mingled in various states of sunburn and spiritual reflection. I was pleasantly shocked by the number of faces I now recognized and even more so that I could remember their names. This was not historically my strong suit. Since my mum's Alzheimer's diagnosis, memory has taken on new meaning. I've become a self-appointed student of neuroplasticity, obsessive consumer of blueberries and walnuts, and now nightly recorder of every pilgrim name I encounter. It's not just about manners. It's about wiring. Preserving. Hoping.

I sat down with the motley crew and was soon trading stories with Mark from Ireland, Ruth from Germany, and Ilze from the Netherlands. Allister and the boys drifted in later, and we all shared dinner together. Beers, laughter, and conversation carried us through the late afternoon, and it was a perfect ending to the day's walk.

I wandered into Santa María Church, a baroque beauty that dominates the town square. That evening, it hosted a 120-year anniversary mass with Spanish liturgy, full choir, and just enough incense to make me feel slightly closer to heaven (or perhaps just mildly intoxicated by sacred smoke). It was magnificent, moving, and mildly soporific. I made it to communion before conceding that my eyelids had unionized against me.

The post-mass procession began at 12:30 am. I had

wanted to stay up to see it, but I opted out. My brain logic dictating that tomorrow's climb trumps tonight's confetti.

TINY PILGRIM TRUTH:

Life doesn't just fill your cup—it teaches you what you're truly thirsty for. And sometimes, it throws in a fly to keep you humble.

CHAPTER 11

CAMINO CONFESSIONS – NO SHAME, JUST RIOJA

September 8 – Day 7: Los Arcos to Logroño (27.8 km)

They say this is the longest walking day on the Camino. Naturally, it was the morning I found myself staring longingly at the luggage taxi leaflet on the nightstand at my pensión. I may not be a practicing Catholic anymore, but I decided that if I were to carry forward any part of that legacy, it would be faith and compassion—not guilt and shame. Especially not the kind that applies to sending one's backpack ahead for a day. So yes, dear reader, I succumbed. No judgment.

Over breakfast, I ran into Alistair and his teenage sons, Aonghus and Charlie, again—our paths clearly synchronizing more than not. I worried briefly about intruding on their family bonding time, but they seemed genuinely delighted to see me. And honestly, if my own 15-year-old had the option of spending the day talking with a stranger rather than his mother, I have no illusions about what he'd choose.

We walked under a sky full of promises the sun didn't quite keep. Cool and overcast, not the glorious Rioja sunshine we were told to expect. But perfect walking weather, really. The scenery gave us rolling vineyards, red clay paths, and a landscape beginning to taste like wine even before a glass was poured. We'd officially entered La Rioja, Spain's most storied wine region. Even the air felt like it had aged in oak.

More than the destination today, I was anticipating the ritual I'd promised myself: tomorrow in Nájera, I would begin reading Mum's Camino journal, the one she started in this very town on September 7, 2012. She had attempted the Camino a year earlier but cut her journey short in Logroño to return home to support my brother through a difficult time.

We are five siblings. Five versions of childhood. Five different mothers, in some ways. Same woman but different windows. She was vibrant, magnetic, deeply loving, and quick with affection. But also complex, exacting, occasionally volatile, and unapologetically stubborn. She and I were alike in all the most combustible ways—effusive, extroverted, affectionate. Ours was an easy relationship, but not always a simple one.

I looked forward to reading her reflections each night after writing my own, tracing the same towns, the same terrain, separated by a decade and a mother-daughter bond that now stretches across memory and disease.

The conversation during today's walk was rich and effortless, and time folded in on itself. I almost forgot I wasn't carrying my pack until I noticed I missed it— that surprising little ache for its weight and its company. There's something oddly beautiful about carrying everything you need on your back. It humbles you. It grounds you. It reminds you how little you require to keep moving forward.

We arrived in Logroño just after 4 PM. This city, once a

strategic Roman outpost and later a medieval trade hub, is now the capital of Rioja.

My pensión was a real study in architectural confusion: with an entrance through a locked street gate, up three elevators, and then down a narrow corridor of cubicle-sized rooms. I took a fast shower and was impatient to escape it.

In contrast, Santa María de la Redonda, the city's grand cathedral (because, of course, it's called Santa María—the Camino's version of "John Smith"), offered a full sensory reset. I stepped inside just as Beethoven was being played live on a colossal pipe organ. The musician, a young man, maybe 20, played with a kind of divine defiance, drawing in locals and pilgrims alike, all standing in stunned silence, mouths half open. It was transcendent.

Later, I found a wine bar and caught up with my family on video calls: Neil, Jordan, and Ryan in San Diego; then Mum in Ireland; and finally my sister. Ten days gone isn't much by any normal standard, but the Camino dilates time. Maybe it's the walking or the intimacy of moving from town to town, self to self. Every step feels like you're walking toward something—even if you don't yet know what.

That evening, I met Alistair and the boys again for a final dinner. Too much Rioja (predictably excellent), too many laughs, and just enough sentiment to make parting feel bittersweet. They were heading to Sarria the next day. Our paths now diverged. How lovely it had been to meet and get to know them.

The Camino has a way of letting people walk in and out of your story at just the right time. And when you're lucky, they leave behind more than a footprint; they leave a thread. I really enjoyed my time with those three and invited the boys to come visit anytime. I had a feeling deep down that I would see them again someday. I hoped so.

I don't remember a single coherent thought as I collapsed into bed that night. I was too tired, maybe a little too tipsy. But the ritual would begin tomorrow. Mum's journal beside mine. Her words, my steps. Her voice, echoing through my own. And somewhere, just maybe, we'll walk this part together. Tomorrow, she would be taking my hand in hers. And already, I felt less lonely.

TINY PILGRIM TRUTH:

We miss the weight not for the strain, but for the strength it revealed in us.

CHAPTER 12

A NEW RITUAL

September 9 - Day 8: Logroño to Nájera (28.9 km)

By all accounts, I should have woken up with a hangover. I earned it one fair and square. But in what I can only describe as a minor Camino miracle, I woke clear-headed, upright, and even vaguely enthusiastic about walking nearly 29km. Perhaps a little Camino miracle? Or perhaps Rioja, at €2 a glass, is simply too noble to punish its devotees.

If my mother were here, she would've started the day with a firm but affectionate:

"Oh, Andy Pet… what on earth were you thinking?" (Said with a head tilt, half a smirk, and zero interest in waiting for an answer.) I doubt she began this stretch of the Camino with a wine headache, but we each walk our own version of the path. Hers was fueled by coffee and sugar. Mine? A little more fermented.

From this chapter forward, I'm introducing a new companion on the trail—my mother's Camino journal. She walked these same steps twelve years ago, beginning in

Logroño in September 2012. Each night, after writing my own entry, I now open hers, read her words, and feel her walking beside me—not just as memory, but as a mirror.

Her voice will travel alongside mine in these chapters—sometimes echoing, sometimes diverging, always meaningful.

The day was long, sunlit, and solitary, just how I wanted it. I walked mostly alone. The trail meandered through vineyards, whispering their ancient secrets, and past sunbaked hills that looked like they had exhaled all their stories centuries ago.

I stopped in Navarrete, a modest but lovely village where I found a church that, in a shocking plot twist, was not named "Santa María." It was the Church of the Assumption—finally, some naming diversity. I had a good coffee, chatted with a few pilgrims, and pressed on.

Arriving in Nájera felt triumphant. This town, once a royal seat of the Kingdom of Navarre, is nestled on the banks of the River Najerilla, its ochre cliffs towering like sentinels. Here, tradition whispers from the stone walls, and you sense you're merely the latest in a long procession of pilgrims to arrive thirsty, dusty, and slightly sunburned.

On entering the town, my eyes were immediately drawn to a cross perched high on a hill. I knew at once I had to climb to it. That urge, I realized, came straight from my father. If there was a castle wall to scramble over, a "do not trespass" sign to ignore, he was there first, drawn to such challenges like a moth to a flame. I am very much the same. And so I climbed the hill. At the top, the reward was well worth the effort. The rooftops of Nájera were bathed in the gold of evening, the river unwinding below like a silver ribbon, and a silence so deep it felt like prayer. I sat down on a fallen log, let the late sun hit my face, and drew a long breath.

Back at the Albergue, a traditional pilgrim hostel, simple and often shared, I joined the 8 p.m. communal dinner. An eight-bed mixed dorm, a €10 dinner, and all the personality you could ask for. I met Becky from Waterford and Megan from San Francisco, both in their late 20s, bright-eyed and blistered. Looking around, I smiled. I was clearly at the kids' table. From an accounting perspective, maybe I belonged at the table behind, but tonight this was exactly where I was meant to be.

Today I met a Canadian woman walking with her 79-year-old mother, and I thought: that could have been us. Mum and me. She couldn't walk beside me now. Alzheimer's has her firmly in its long shadows, but in every step, I still felt her close. Asking for coffee. Laughing at my hangover. Holding my hand at the hilltop. Physically, she remained strong as an ox, and maybe a year or two earlier, she could have managed it. But Alzheimer's, diagnosed four years ago (though we suspect it had been creeping in for much longer, hidden behind "old-age" jokes and post-chemo fog), erodes the body as much as the mind. And so here I was, walking for both of us. I despised what Alzheimer's had stolen and continued to steal.

But I am deeply grateful for what her journey has given me: words on paper and her steps to follow.

Mum's Journal

Walked alone. Difficulty finding the route from the hotel. Good breakfast in Logroño—I was heeding Barbara's lectures on food. Three coffee stops only. At the third, I met Brazilian and Swedish girls. Walked with them. Too hot and five kilometers too long. Lovely Albergue in Nájera on the water. Dinner with the Brazilian. I want to walk alone tomorrow.

Her entry made me smile. The coffee rationing (her version of discipline), the quick companionship, and that very human note: "5 km too long." She was 68 when she walked this; I was 50. There's a lot of wear-and-tear difference in 18 years.

I understood, deeply, her desire to walk alone. Many of us do. There's something sacred in solitude—in the space to hear your thoughts finish themselves. The Camino has a way of moving through your body first, then your mind, and finally, if you let it, your soul.

TINY PILGRIM TRUTH:

"Grief walks beside us, but so does love, and love knows the way."

CHAPTER 13

THE HEN, THE PARADOUR, AND THE HALF-IRON MAN MIC DROP

September 10 - Day 9: Najera to Santo Domingo de la Calzada (21.3 km)

I left Najera under the cover of darkness, guided more by caffeine instinct than by headlamp. My reward: a croissant and coffee at a riverside café that had the decency to open before sunrise. Praise be.

As the sun teased the hills awake, I struck up a conversation with Kim, a delightfully chatty South Korean pilgrim whose energy could have powered the Camino's entire scallop shell supply chain. We parted ways in the charming village of Azofra, where my second coffee of the morning was accompanied by a chorus of accents and laughter. There, I bumped into the brother and sister duo, Michael and Stephanie, from Australia. Stephanie's husband was tag-teaming this Camino leg with her, one day walking alone and the other accompanying their injured daughter on the bus to the next town. Michael had joined for a week after a wedding in Greece and was now wishing he were doing it all.

We walked together for a stretch, trading stories, laughs, and sunblock, the countryside rolling beside us in warm, lazy waves of farmland. There was a less poetic stretch along a main road just before Santo Domingo, but we tapped into a very Camino trait and forgave it. Lunch with Michael and Stephanie was lovely, and they insisted on picking up the tab. I have a soft spot for the kind of people you practically need to arm-wrestle to let you pay the bill.

We hugged goodbye, knowing they'd be half a day ahead from now on. I'd miss their company but was secretly thrilled because tonight, tonight, I had a reservation at a Parador. For the uninitiated, a Parador is Spain's way of saying, "You've earned it, dear pilgrim." Imagine: a centuries-old palace or monastery turned luxury hotel, starched white sheets, double beds, bathrobes with actual dignity, and a tub that could baptize away every sore muscle.

Naturally, I ran a bath, lit a mental candle, and dissolved. I napped for twenty minutes, then stared at the bed like it was a Monet. I considered a second nap, but this was Santo Domingo de la Calzada—and I was ready to explore.

Santo Domingo de la Calzada is a town steeped in history and medieval charm, named after Saint Dominic of the Causeway, who devoted his life to making the Camino safer by building roads, bridges, and, most famously, this very town. But what really captures the imagination is the legend of the hanged innocent and the resurrected chicken.

Here's the tale. A young German pilgrim traveling with his parents caught the eye of a noble girl, who fell madly for him. When he did not return her affection, she sought revenge. As the family left town, she accused him of theft. Wrongly charged, he was condemned and hanged. His devastated parents prayed at Saint Dominic's tomb, and when they returned to the gallows, they found their son alive, still hanging, saved, it seemed, by divine grace. Rushing to tell the magistrate of the miracle, they were met with scorn. He sneered, "Your son is no more alive than this roast chicken on my plate." At which point the chicken leapt up and crowed.

And so, to this day, a live hen and rooster are kept inside the Cathedral of Santo Domingo de la Calzada, a rotating pair of feathered legends-in-residence. I climbed the steps behind the altar (with the caretaker's blessing), and there they were. Living proof that the Camino, like faith, always leaves room for magic.

As I wandered the city's cobbled lanes, Jordan called.

She was in Galway, just after saying goodbye to Mum, after her summer-long stay in Galway. Their bond has always been beautiful. Mum was part grandmother, part fairy godmother. This might be the last time Mum would know her. They've always had a bond that was so close. Mum was the kind of grandmother who took the grandkids on an overnight build your shelter experience in an Irish forest at 69, scripted, choreographed and hosted a children's play, complete with costumes, and an invited audience of bewildered neighbors. She didn't just babysit. She created worlds.

While my voice stayed steady on the phone, something in me buckled. Every day feels like a small goodbye, I thought. I listened and then did what any other mother would do: I tried to offer some words of comfort. I reassured her: these moments, these wild, wonderful memories, no disease could erase them. And although Mum will forget them, Jordan will not. They were her inheritance.

By dinner, I was emotionally spent, physically knackered,

and ravenous. I stumbled into what I thought was a humble tavern, only to see the Michelin plaque after I'd sat down. Oh well, I smiled, *this will have to do*. Classic me. A what in Ireland you could call a fine strapping man from Carlow, whom I'd passed on the trail earlier, was seated alone nearby. I wasn't madly in the mood to talk, but given the restaurant was entirely empty at this point, bar the two of us, we were a bread bun throw away, and we were facing each other, it would have been more awkward not to. I caught his attention and invited him to join me with a zero-pressure escape clause. He accepted.

He was quiet, kind, generous, and quietly good company —interested and curious. I had initially pegged him as an introvert, though to be fair, almost everyone seems introverted when sitting next to me. Still, our conversation unfolded with an easy rhythm, free of awkward pauses or over-rehearsed anecdotes.

Born a farmer and still shaped by it with broad hands, square shoulders, a thick country accent, and a quiet steadiness, he turned out, somewhat surprisingly, to be both a serial entrepreneur and a seasoned traveler. There's nothing better than when a person surprises you by being the exact opposite of what you assumed. I try not to sort people too quickly, though I know it's a tendency I still wrestle with. We are so quick to try to label people. I was intrigued by his diverse business ventures. Inflatable castles and vaping supplies. I blinked. "That's... quite the combo," I said, trying not to imagine one business inflating the other.

I could see him unclenching as the night went on, his reserve giving way to something warmer, easier. He spoke with a kind of bashful bravado about finishing his first sprint triathlon just a few months back—trying to play it cool, but the pride leaked through every word. Then he asked, almost offhand, "You know what a sprint triathlon is?"

I paused for just a beat, smiled, and took a slow sip of Rioja, trying not to look too smug but enjoying the delicious moment of understatement. "Funny you ask," I said. "I just did my first Half Ironman."

His eyebrows shot up. Mine stayed politely in place. For a brief, perfect moment, we were simply equals at that table, two Irish pilgrims raising our glasses. He, with his Coke, the "non-drinking" farmer-turned-entrepreneur and triathlete; me, with my Rioja, the ex-corporate techie, part fashionista, part frequent flyer, now trading heels for hiking shoes.

That's the Camino for you. It throws together the most mismatched souls and makes them kin. We laughed about our very "un-pilgrim" evening and parted ways beneath the stars outside our respective Paradors. He said he was trying to quit smoking. That, it turned out, wasn't entirely true. But the beauty of the Camino is that no explanation is required. You don't need a tragic backstory or a lofty purpose to walk. The road makes room for all of us, whether we're chasing miracles, chasing fitness, or simply chasing a good Rioja.

That night, wrapped in linen and warmth, I opened Mum's journal.

Mum's journal entry

Started with the Brazilians, but then went ahead. Only just 20km. Feel like it's a doddle. Roasting hot. Lovely countryside. Saw there was a Cistercian abbey Albergue, and went in there. Oh God. Rotten nun behind what looked like bulletproof glass. I am exhausted. Tiny room, loads of beds. Met American Mum and Daughter, Dianne and Hillary, who want me to see a doctor about my cut toe. Put plaster on. All good. Dinner with them and go for a quick walk and an early night. Also met a Dutch man in Azofra—walked from Holland with a tent. I'm not so mad after all.

Her words are so sparse—like she was being charged by the syllable. Maybe she was just knackered. Or maybe, 18 years older than I am now, she didn't have the luxury of flowery introspection. But she still found a connection. Kindness. Story. Much like I did today.

As I turned off the light, I felt a twinge of guilt for my plush Parador, while she braved bunk beds and blistered toes. But I swear I could hear her voice in my head, warm and amused: "Of course you would, my darling."

And with that, I slept. Hen legend, Ironman ego, Michelin menu and all.

TINY PILGRIM TRUTH:

Every now and then, the Camino weaves a little extra wonder into the ordinary—and you realize it wasn't an ordinary day at all.

CHAPTER 14

OF PINK POLKA DOTS AND PILGRIMAGE

Sept 11 - Day 10: Santo Domingo to Belorado (21.3 km)

This morning, I lingered. When you sleep in pressed white sheets in a 12th-century former convent, now a Parador, it feels almost criminal to rise before the sun. So I didn't. I sauntered down to the grand buffet at 8:30 a.m., sampled everything, and made off with contraband bread and cheese wrapped in a linen napkin, feeling a little like "Oliver Twist."

At breakfast, I met Mary Beth, a federal judge from Boston with a wicked sense of humor and a command of case law that could turn a pilgrim's breakfast into a Senate hearing. We talked about motherhood, ambition, and the beautiful blur of both. By 9:30 a.m., I finally hit the trail.

This morning called for music. Not podcasts. Not silence. Music. And not just any music—ABBA. It was inevitable, almost ancestral. My mother played their albums on loop while pregnant with me, believing (without scientific backing but with a mother's certainty) that the sound waves of "Dancing Queen" would shape a joyful child. It might've worked. The moment "Mamma Mia" played, I wasn't just listening; I was remembering the first soundtrack of my life.

Mum was a pistol. A legend. Decades ahead of her time. And, if I'm being honest, I've spent most of my life trying to be just like her.

She parented with a flair for the dramatic and a heart full of generosity. One of her greatest hits? The midnight feast. At about 9 p.m. on random nights, I'd scribble a note—"Dear Mum, we are starving." I'd dispatch my youngest brother as the courier. Moments later, she'd arrive upstairs, arms full of biscuits, or crisps and orange juice, and enough fanfare to rival a royal banquet. No other mother in Galway was staging Narnia-level snacks on a Tuesday night. But mine did.

She could be pure magic, and she made you feel like you were magic, too.

Of course, she had her flaws. She could be fiery, stubborn, a hurricane in a leopard-print scarf. But on days like today, I didn't want to catalog her contradictions; I just wanted to walk with the memory of her laughter echoing between my steps.

By late afternoon, I stumbled into the tiny village of Belorado, sun-drunk and ready to collapse. My reward? A charming Albergue (think "hostel with soul," complete with a pool, a pizza, and a cold beer). I devoured all three. Then came an hour of chatting with a cheerful band of Irish pilgrims who were tipsy, kind, and full of stories. Classic.

At sunset, I had a massage that sent me into a deep coma. Then I curled up with my mother's journal. And there it was—Belorado. She stayed in this same place, maybe even this room. I read her words again, as if she were writing them to me, not just about her day but into mine.

Very hot. Set out alone. Easy most of the way. Met all nationalities and ages. Someone at a coffee shop told me there was an Irishman about, so I went and said hi to Peter from Westport. Very friendly. Went on alone. All great. But the last 3 km felt like 100. Came to the Albergue with a restaurant and pool just before Belorado. Ate with Peter when he arrived. Had dinner with him, Warren, and Hamish. Later, sat out with them having a drink overlooking the countryside. Magical. Met Nekana in the next bunk bed. Tomorrow seems difficult due to the heat, so I decided to send heavy bags ahead. I have 582 km left to Santiago. Saving energy.

I read her words under crisp white sheets, imagining her in the same spot, same village, maybe even the same bunk. It was as if she reached through time, past memory loss and silence, and laid her hand on mine.

No encounter is by chance. Not the strangers, not the detours, not the journals tucked into our backpacks. I'm beginning to understand: as I meet new people, I'm also meeting new parts of myself—and rediscovering hers.

TINY PILGRIM TRUTH:

Sometimes, the most sacred encounters aren't with strangers but with memories that arrive just in time.

CHAPTER 15

THE SNORER, THE SAINT, AND THE VANISHING YORKSHIREMAN

September 12 - Day 11: Belorado to San Juan de Ortega (24.5 km)

We left Belorado before dawn, the town still dreaming. I'd just had the best sleep of the trip in a four-bed room. Over breakfast, I bumped into Shawn, my Kiwi roommate, who had set out even earlier in a bid to escape the nocturnal wrath of an elderly Dutch woman whose snoring, he claimed, had vibrated the stone walls.

Shawn had tweaked his knee, but you wouldn't have guessed it. He kept telling me to go ahead if he slowed down, but to be honest, he never did. I eased my pace slightly, without making a thing of it, but I was genuinely impressed. I couldn't help but wonder what he'd be like uninjured. Possibly Olympic? I kept reminding him to slow down. He didn't. Typical. Male hearing is, I have learned, excellent for things like sports scores, but selectively impaired for suggestions.

The morning mist clung to the trees as we wound our way

through forest trails and rolling hills. It was quiet, lush, and humid enough to give your clothes personality. After two charming coffee stops (both entirely necessary), I ran into Michael from Australia. He'd missed a bus and was weighing up his next move. I offered to pray for divine intervention. He laughed. We both knew that heaven likely doesn't prioritize missed transport connections.

The final stretch brought a steep, stony climb and a beautiful reward: San Juan de Ortega. This place isn't really a town; it's a whisper of one. A monastery, a 12th-century church, one bar, and a hostel that feels like a medieval sleepover experiment. The exterior of the monastery is striking; the inside is best described as "piously falling apart." For €15, I landed a coveted lower bunk (a small but mighty victory) in a cavernous dorm of forty strangers. I never imagined I would write that sentence! Years of Hyatt and Marriott Suites had done little to prepare me for this kind of "accommodation."

Post-shower and sink laundry, I joined Shawn for lemon beer and paella. Later, I shared tea with Hetty, a radiant Dutch woman whose warmth wrapped around you like a soft shawl. At 6 p.m., we joined pilgrims from around the world for Mass in the ancient church, standing where thousands have stood across a millennium. San Juan de Ortega, a disciple of Saint Dominic, had built this place to protect pilgrims on what was once the most dangerous stretch of the Camino. He chose service as his legacy. Kindness carved into limestone.

Dinner was in the monastery's great hall, served communally. I splurged and bought three bottles of red wine (€24), a gesture met with cheers and roars. Pilgrims toasted me like a minor saint. Wine, it turns out, is the universal love language.

The conversation meandered into politics, philosophy, and

then, inevitably, British eccentricity. Adrian from Yorkshire delivered a jaw-droppingly outdated take on contraception and women's rights. Despite a marathon of words, he never managed to explain why he was so staunchly opposed to such a modern, necessary invention. I responded with what I believed was a polite counterpoint — though my raised eyebrow may have said more than my words. He promptly excused himself for the restroom and never returned. Whether he was offended or fell prey to 12th-century plumbing, I suppose I'll never know. Either way, I choose to believe it was divine intervention.

The night ended cold and damp, but sweet. Shawn, forever the Kiwi gentleman, gave me his spare blanket and one of his earplugs. Before I could say "thank you," I was already asleep.

Mum's Journal

I set out with Warren. No bags today. Beautiful walk. Great fun. Feeling guilty about sending bags ahead. I really didn't need to, it's hilly but not difficult. Coffee in Villafranca and met Anna from Germany again, and we walked together. At the top of the hill (beside the Monument), I set off alone and got lost among the wind turbines. I met a helmeted guy in a truck on a narrow path and stopped him. Yes, confirmed, I am on the wrong route. He kindly gave me a lift back to the correct path. It's a beautiful walk through the woods. St Juan is tiny and cute, but with NO luggage. A Danish lady gave me new underwear. Nekana gave me a loan of her used towel (wet) and some shampoo. Went to mass in the old, beautiful church. Ben phoned. Glass of wine with the Danish lady. Went for a walk and bed at 8:15 pm.

There's something magical about knowing I stood where

she stood, drank coffee in the same plazas, and watched the light hit the same monastery walls.

When I told Mum I was walking the Camino, she lit up with joy. Then she forgot five minutes later. But the strange grace of Alzheimer's is that good news is always new. Every time I remind her, she lights up again. The Camino never gets old.

Today, like every other day, I walked not just for myself, but for her. For the parts of her that are fading and the pieces of her I'm collecting as I go. For the reminder that grace, like kindness, often comes from strangers, soup, and shared silence.

TINY PILGRIM TRUTH:

Not all saints wear robes. Some bring you beer, a spare blanket, or listen when you need to be heard, even if they're limping alongside you.

CHAPTER 16

LOST POLES, FOUND PEOPLE, AND THE SPIRITUAL GEOMETRY OF SUNFLOWERS

September 13 - Day 12: San Juan de Ortega to Burgos (26.1 km)

I may have had the best sleep of my entire adult life in a room with 40 strangers, lumpy bunk beds, and the lingering scent of damp hiking socks. Consider me officially, bona fide, a pilgrim. Maybe I was just really tired. Either way, I woke at 9 a.m., which on the Camino is basically slothful teenager territory, and somehow slept through 40 pilgrims rising, packing, and disappearing. That's not rapture; that's exhaustion.

But someone had left their walking poles behind. So naturally, I appointed myself the Camino Saint of Lost Gear and carried them with me in hopes of reuniting them with their rightful owner. And yes, I imagined the eventual handoff would involve tears, applause, and possibly a nomination for sainthood.

The walk into Burgos was long but beautiful. Once, the silence of the Camino came not from leading but from following — and I welcomed it. I passed through still woods and golden sunflower fields stretching like an ocean of joy. At one point, I carved a smiley face into a sunflower head, its little seeds falling easily out. That's how I felt. Happy. Unburdened. Maybe just high on sleep and gratitude.

About halfway through, I reached the Cruz de Matagrand, a humble iron cross but a powerful symbol. I paused. I breathed deeply. The Camino was slowing me down, not in pace but in presence. When your only responsibilities are walking, eating, and sleeping, and when conversations are spontaneous, raw, and refreshingly agenda-free, you start syncing to a different rhythm. And that rhythm starts to feel more like, well, more like you.

I hadn't seen anyone ahead for some time, but eventually spotted a lone figure. Camino etiquette says you can pass with just a "Buen Camino," but there's this strange, almost magnetic pull toward certain people, like your internal compass quietly whispering, "Her. Walk with her."

Her name was Jackie, from L.A. She was limping, struggling, and clearly weighing the decision to quit. She'd planned this journey for months and spent most of her savings to be here. And yet, her body was threatening to betray her. But that wasn't the worst of it.

A kilometer or so later, she told me her story. Two years ago, her husband died of pancreatic cancer. The day after his death, she found out via his phone that he'd been having multiple affairs. She had to host the funeral, manage the condolences, and carry that private storm in silence. Her pain was still raw, barely contained beneath her smile. I listened. Something had brought her here. Maybe walking would help her legs, but the journey? The journey might help her heart. She was a woman of deep faith and still desperately wanted to get to Santiago. I hoped deeply that she would get there.

Closer to Burgos, the charm gave way to concrete. An industrial sprawl that looked like it had been designed by someone actively protesting joy. I stopped at a grim diner for a coffee that tasted like existential despair, and as I left, I spotted familiar faces from the monastery. "Anyone missing some poles?" I called out.

Peter jumped three feet in the air. "My poles!" he shouted, hugging them like a long-lost pet. Good deed: achieved. Halo status: pending.

Burgos itself? Stunning. The Plaza Mayor felt like something out of a painting, with colorful buildings in hues of blue, yellow, red, and orange framing the breezy square. "Rainbow Plaza" would've been a better name, honestly. I sat with a tinto de verano and a fully loaded beef "Burgo," soaking it all in.

Later, I checked into my delightfully clean pension (no bunk beds!), wandered the winding streets, and visited the magnificent Burgos Cathedral. It's a Gothic marvel with spires that look like they were plucked straight from a fantasy novel. Inside? Twenty-eight chapels. Twenty-eight! It's basically a small country disguised as a church.

I ran into Henk, my Presbyterian friend from the Netherlands, and we strolled and talked theology. He's the kind of man who can make you see stained glass differently. Eventually, he left in pursuit of socks, and I climbed to the hilltop castle ruins, took in the city view, and let myself marvel at how far I had come.

That night, I met a rowdy, lovable crew, many of whom would later become true Camino friends. There was Bianca from Australia—emotional, very tipsy, with a flair for the dramatic. Richard, dubbed King Richard, and Tim from the UK. I liked Tim instantly. He was equal parts wit and warmth. Mark from Ireland. Olivier from Canada. Ruth from Germany. It was pizza, beer, and laughter. But as they went off for more revelry, I quietly slipped away. I wasn't ready to belong to a group just yet. The Camino still needed me on its own terms. So, I "Irish-exited" my way into solitude and sleep.

Tomorrow: the Meseta. Some love it; some hate it. Everyone has an opinion. But tonight, I curled up with my now-favorite ritual.

Mum's Journal

No bags still. I need it now. Leave alone incredibly early. Pitch dark. So beautiful, out of the village and into the woods. A quarter moon and a few stars. Open fields in early light and fields of sunflowers, and then cows, and miraculously, I was not afraid. I met Anna and walked a few kilometers with her. She reminds me of Ben, so gentle and free-spirited. At the Burgos industrial estate, I took the bus to the center. No bags there either. Have a glass of wine, lovely in Burgos, walk to the hostel; huge and really nice beside the magnificent cathedral. Dinner with Warren and Anne Marie (Scotland). Sleeping so well...

P.S. Got bags later; had to walk another 3–4 km to another hostel for them.

I read her words that night, curled up in my private room, and felt a wave of quiet kinship. Our days mirrored each other more than I expected—sunflowers, wine, wonder, misdirection, and moments of grace. But what struck me most wasn't just where we both walked—it was how we walked. With curiosity. With resilience. With an openness to whatever the day would bring.

TINY PILGRIM TRUTH:

Sometimes the person you're meant to walk with is a stranger. And sometimes, it's someone you've loved your whole life, waiting for you in the pages of a journal.

CHAPTER 17

LOSING THE WAY, FINDING THE WONDER

September 14- Day 13: Burgos to Hornillos del Camino (20.9 km)

This morning, I was slow to rise. Not physically wrecked, exactly, though my feet had opinions, but emotionally low. Maybe that's just what happens on Day 13 of walking across a country with nothing but your thoughts, a backpack, and your own existential hum.

I rolled out of bed in my tidy little pension and began the daily Camino shuffle: stretch, repack, mutter, repeat. But something was missing: my Camino guidebook. My trusty, battered, pocket-sized pilgrimage partner. This wasn't just a guidebook; it was my analog compass, my daily ritual, my security blanket with elevation maps. I turned my bag inside out. Nothing.

I could feel a minor spiritual crisis en route.

But then I remembered my mum's words from her own Camino: "Things are rarely lost for good." She'd once left her pilgrim passport in a café, only to have it returned by kind strangers shouting her name at her hostel. She and my grandmother, both pragmatists to the bone and only religious when required, swore by one Hail Mary fix-all: St. Anthony, patron saint of lost things.

So I prayed. Half-skeptical, half-desperate. It was only 7:30 a.m., and the restaurant where I'd last used it didn't open until 9:00. Camino logic dictated I crawl back into bed, so I did. Honestly, I think even St. Anthony would've approved.

At 9:00 sharp, I walked into the café and was greeted with: "Señora, ¿su libro?" My Camino book was safe behind the counter. I could've kissed the bartender for a few reasons, but mostly because of the book. Instead, I left a generous tip and walked out grinning like a lunatic, croissant in one hand and coffee in the other. The Camino provides.

Today marked my official entry into the Meseta, a vast, golden plateau that Camino pilgrims either fall in love with or loathe entirely. I fell hard. The landscape stretched endlessly with gold wheat dancing under a cobalt sky. It was silence and space and stillness. The world had flattened out, and so had my thoughts. I was alone, but loneliness couldn't keep up. The Camino had stripped everything down to its essentials: Walk. Breathe. Notice.

At the village of Rabé, I ordered a beer and a soup at 11 a.m., a combination that made little sense on any menu. But I wanted them both. And that's the thing about life: sometimes the pairings that look absurd end up satisfying. Then I ducked into a tiny chapel, Ermita de Nuestra Señora de Monasterio, where an elderly nun with a face like an angel and the hands of a wise grandmother asked for my pilgrim passport. She stamped it, smiled, and placed her hands gently on my head to offer a blessing. She placed a simple thread with a small silver medallion over my head. In that instant, something moved inside me—wordless and undeniable.

Then, instantly and unexpectedly, my eyes welled up. Tears came, unbidden, streaming down my face.

Later, walking with Pavarotti and Bocelli in my ears, the Meseta opened wide before me. Butterflies flitted through the sunflowers. A surprise grove of trees appeared like an oasis, a half kilometer off the path, and whispered, "rest here." So I did. I leaned against a huge bark, closed my eyes, and napped under a cathedral of branches. I had always wanted to do that and wasn't sure why it had taken fifty years.

In Hornillos, I reunited with Ruth from Germany and met a sweet Aussie named Loughly. We shared a bottle of wine on the curb outside the hostel, one of those impromptu moments that feel bigger than they are. They were light, sociable, and enjoyable company. Later, I bumped into Jackie from L.A., who was still wrestling with whether to continue.

We both ran into Kim from Colorado, who's walked the Camino three times and recently published a book about it. We sat outside a bar that randomly played Guns N' Roses (the Meseta doesn't do predictability), and Jackie opened up again.

She was still unsure. The pain, both physical and emotional, clung to her, and the doubts never left. Kim and I knew instinctively that what she needed was quiet company, not speeches or silver linings. Sometimes that's all anyone needs: space to sit with the ache, and company that doesn't rush, judge, or try to mend what isn't ready to heal. When she asked for my thoughts as we wrapped up the evening, I told her the only thing any of us can do: take it one day at a time. She probably never imagined she'd make it this far, and yet here she was. I reminded her I'd heard how much she wanted to reach Santiago. And if she couldn't walk every mile because of injury or exhaustion, there were still other ways to get there. No matter what you do, I said, get to Santiago. You deserve to see it.

That night, back at the Albergue, I had a video call with Neil and Ryan, my two boys back home. I missed them more than I expected, and their faces grounded me.

As I curled into my lower bunk, I reflected on what I loved most about the Camino: the conversations. People don't talk from their heads here. They talk from the heart. And that changes everything.

I opened Mum's journal.

Mum's journal entry

Set out at 7 am. Long way out of Burgos, busy roads. Coffee en route and meet Gerry (Dutch Camper), and then set off alone again. Into the Meseta now. This is my favourite part. All gold through the crop fields. Met David, appropriately named "Short Shorts" from Dublin. Sad man. He, unfortunately, takes great interest in me (my luck)! Complains about not getting Australian and Irish Pensions. His 5th Camino. I ask why—wondering if I will even do one—and he answers, "the sky (free heat), cheap food, drink and accommodation." Oh God, please let him disappear. But no one answers my prayer.

I get to a cute village, but notice I have lost my Camino book and passport. I am really upset. One hour later, two Spanish men came into the hostel and called my name. They found them on the road out of Burgos. Other people told me they stopped at all stops along the way, calling out my name. So thrilled—hug them and drag them for a quick drink in the only pub in the village. They are walking into the next village.

Such kindness. But no sleep in the horrible Albergue. I actually fell out of the top bunk at 3 am and really hurt my hands and knees. Tomorrow will be interesting. Bottom bunks really should be reserved for people of a "certain age."

I smiled as I read her words. So many overlaps I hadn't expected. We both lost our Camino books on the same stretch. We both had them returned by strangers who went out of their way to help. Different years, different journeys, but somehow, we were tripping over the same moments. It didn't feel like a coincidence. It felt like a quiet thread tying us together, one village at a time. We both loved the Meseta.

TINY PILGRIM TRUTH:

Losing something on the Camino can feel like chaos. Finding it again feels like grace. What happens in between? That's where the learning lives.

CHAPTER 18

FALLING IN LOVE WITH THE MESETA

September 15 - Day 14: Hornillos to Castrojeriz (20.1 km)

God, I love the Meseta.

After a surprisingly good sleep in an overcrowded Albergue filled with creaking bunk beds and the occasional melodic snore, I ducked out early, opting to skip breakfast when I saw "margarine" on the table. For an Irish girl, this was sacrilege.

As the sun rose, the Meseta was blanketed in shimmering gold, and I was in heaven. I walked for a while with Kim from Colorado, then we were joined by Locky and his friend Peter from Australia. Peter, a very young but still retired cop, had survived a near-fatal gunshot and a hit-and-run incident in the line of duty. His body was now held together by bolts and screws, but his spirit was light. As he told his story, you could feel the gratitude reverberate through him. It was awe-inspiring.

Somewhere along the way, between the heavenly sunrise and the stirring conversation, I realized it had been five days since I'd… well… had a proper "movement." A condition my bunkmate Chris from Ohio dubbed "The Great Out-of-Town Shut-Down." When I relayed this charming fact to my daughter Jordan, soon-to-be med student, she proposed, with mock-clinical seriousness, "Mum, maybe you're just burning more calories than you're eating… so there's literally nothing to come out." A diagnosis both horrifying and… weirdly flattering? Either way, I chose to believe her. Nothing like a little GI crisis to make you feel like an elite athlete.

We passed through a deep valley and then, suddenly, the town of Hontanas appeared out of nowhere. There was a holy well near a statue of Saint Bridget of Sweden, inviting pilgrims to refill their flasks and wash their hands. Feeling unexpectedly virtuous, I obliged.

In the distance, the ghostly ruins of the Convent of San Antón emerged, all crumbling ashlars and Gothic arches. The place radiated a sacred, mysterious energy. Beneath a massive oak—over 1,000 years old, if legend is to be believed—I rested, breathed, and absolutely felt the presence of something greater than myself.

Later that day, I practically skipped into Castrojeriz, giddy at the promise of something wildly un-Camino: a 5-star hotel. "The San Francisco" was its name, and it did not disappoint. The garden was an aromatic feast of herbs and blossoms, and I let my feet bask in a cold pool before submitting to a blissful head massage.

Lunch was paella with friends. I saw Ed from Carlow checking in and recommended the massage with a five-star review sort of wink. Then, as sunset neared, I set off solo again, climbing the steep hill to the castle overlooking town.

The view was majestic. I wondered if Mum had made it up here; it was quite the climb.

Most pilgrims crash into their bunks by sundown, maybe squeezing in a beer and a plate of something fried. But me? If there was a hill to climb, a castle to discover, or a half-hidden museum, I was there. The day wasn't done while curiosity outran common sense.

Dinner was a beautiful organic meal back at the hotel, where I met Perry and Chris, two Australians walking the Camino in memory of their 28-year-old daughter who had died tragically just a year earlier. The grief in their eyes was unspeakable, etched in every glance, every pause. It made my own heart hurt.

Later that night, I reached for Mum's journal.

Mum's journal entry

I bought a new lamp from a man in an ancient "sells everything" kind of store. He is gorgeous, in his late 80s. Endlessly helpful, he spends about 20 minutes trying to fix my broken light before selling me a new one. How refreshing! Was this another planet? I met loads of people I know here. The Albergue is volunteer-run; a beautiful young "holy" man type is there. He exudes warmth and kindness. It's a joy. There's a lovely atmosphere with candles burning, and I sleep like a log. This lovely village used to house 200 people; now, only 40 live here.

As I close my eyes, I think about the thousands of mothers over the centuries who watched their children leave small towns like this in search of bigger, better lives. I think about leaving Ireland in 1995—about Mum standing at the Shannon Airport departure gate, not knowing how long I'd be gone.

I had to leave. I had classic small-island fever. Immigration was a rite of passage for the Irish. But I also left to escape the shadows of my parents' messy divorce, Mum's lingering anger, and the pain of words that were said—and never unsaid.

I was angry with her for the things I saw that I shouldn't have, for the bitterness that clung to our home like damp in the walls. I was angry with myself for always trying to fix it, for being the bridge in a house split down the middle.

But I couldn't fix their lives.

All I could do and did was build my own.

And maybe that's the truest thing any of us can do.

Tonight, I give thanks for a soft bed, a clear sky, and for the long road that led me to this point—one footstep, one heartbreak, one holy well at a time.

TINY PILGRIM TRUTH:

What a gift it is to still want to see more, do more, feel more, long after others have called it a day.

CHAPTER 19

THE HILL, THE HOUND, AND THE HIDDEN LANGUAGE OF THE CAMINO

September 16 - Day 15: Castrojeriz to Frómista (24.9 km)

I lingered in my five-star sanctuary in Castrojeriz longer than any pilgrim "should," but I didn't care. After weeks of bunk beds and coin showers, there was something healing about hot coffee, soft sheets, and being looked after, if only for a morning. I left around 9 a.m., deeply grateful and properly fortified, which was essential because the day began with a climb that felt nearly vertical.

On the way up, I met Diane from Canada: confident, candid, and completely magnetic. I'd planned to do a polite flyby, but she had that compelling, truth-telling sparkle. At 65, she was a fierce hiker with even fiercer views on life and love. She had four marriages under her belt, which made her, by her own admission, either supremely qualified or tragically disqualified from giving relationship advice. I joked that both were probably true. We laughed hard. The kind of laughter you don't expect mid-sweat on a Spanish hill.

Later, I dipped my toes into a cool river. It was such a

welcome break after a big climb and a hot day. It was so peaceful. This kind of moment would slip by unnoticed at home. But out here, walking all day with nothing but your thoughts, even the smallest things start to feel special. Maybe that's what walking does: it slows you down just enough to see the beauty that's always been there.

Frómista emerged from the Meseta like a sleepy little sigh, quiet, sun-warmed, and proud of its gem, the Iglesia de San Martín. A marvel of Romanesque architecture, its symmetry and stillness stood in contrast to a quiet moment just outside town.

I saw a young man sitting in the dust, three gigantic wolfish dogs curled protectively around him. He was barefoot, sun-weathered, and clearly making his way to Santiago, sleeping under the stars. We exchanged a few words, his English as bad as my Spanish. His dogs didn't just guard him; they knew him. It was so beautiful to observe. I handed him €20, and he looked up at me, not surprised, not desperate, just deeply grateful. I walked away feeling a little changed, without knowing exactly how or why.

That night, I had dinner with a motley and wonderful crew of Camino friends, including Sonya from Dublin. We clinked glasses, swapped stories, and I collapsed into bed early, full in heart and belly.

Mum's Journal

Have breakfast of sorts in the hostel. Set off alone in darkness. Through the village, downhill, out towards a steep climb to 900m. Can't find a Camino arrow, so wait for the next walker from Korea, and he runs ahead and confirms. Off I go. It's very steep but equally beautiful. What a joy when daylight comes and the Meseta is before me again. It's very cold. I meet Peter, who is frozen in an Irish "ganzy" and has no jacket. Typical Irish. We meet a coffee vendor with a cart on the side of the road. Bliss.

Some people come to the Camino looking for clarity. Others to escape it. Mum, ever the pragmatist, never talked about transformation. She didn't write about lessons or revelations, only what she saw and who she met. Reading her words now, I realize she didn't need to explain herself. She lived it. She walked it. And in her quiet way, she always left room for mystery.

TINY PILGRIM TRUTH

There's a kind of magic in walking, in how it turns the smallest moments into something you feel in your bones.

CHAPTER 20

THE PEACE OFFERING AND THE POWER OF BEING SEEN

September 16- Day 15: Frómista to Carrión de los Condes (20km)

It was still dark when I slipped out of the Albergue, hoping not to wake anyone with the creak of my boots or the clack of the door. There was, tragically, no coffee in sight and out of the shadows, the landlady appeared and called after me: "Buen Camino!" I couldn't help but smile. Still no coffee, but at least my heart was warm.

Luckily, five minutes later, I stumbled upon a quaint little café and bakery. Salvation in a steaming mug. Camino magic strikes again.

The day's walk was a flat one, mostly along the senda, a gravel path running parallel to the main road that many pilgrims moan about. Admittedly, it's not the most scenic or soulful stretch. The landscape is stark, repetitive, and brutally exposed. But for reasons I can't quite explain, I loved it. The clouds above raced across the sky like they were late for something, casting silver shadows on the ever golden Meseta.

At Villalcázar de Sirga, I made a pit stop at the famous Templar church, adorned with crosses and carvings that made my inner history nerd giddy. For a moment, I was no longer a tired pilgrim but felt I was a key character in The Da Vinci Code and part of some secret society. I have always loved history, and this type of history, with all its symbolism and mystery, was fascinating to me.

Back on the path, the wind picked up, and I pulled my buff tight around my face, only to spot Adrian from Yorkshire. Yes, that Adrian with his antiquated contraception views from back in San Juan de Ortega, planted on a rock, changing his socks. Our last encounter had been a mildly heated theological debate, and I wasn't sure if I should slow down, speed up, or fake a phone call to avoid him. But this is the Camino: no exits, no hiding. Just face it. Practice for life.

To my surprise, he looked up and said, "I owe you an apology."

I didn't need it, but I appreciated it. He admitted, in his very British way, that perhaps his views on contraception were "a touch outdated." Translation: wildly prehistoric. I accepted the gesture, and at the next village, he bought me a fresh orange juice and croissant, a Camino peace offering if ever there was one. We walked together for a while until he gasped, "Your pace is going to kill me," and I peeled off with a wave. Pilgrimage diplomacy: successful.

I arrived in Carrión de los Condes by noon and checked into the most charming pension, complete with a private attic room that made me feel like a bohemian artist. After lunch in the square with Ilze and a somewhat overconfident Brit named John, I returned to my room for a massage. At one point, she said, "You have a very strong body." How odd, I initially thought, having never had a masseuse comment on my body stateside. But how refreshing, too.

"Thank you," I replied—and meant it. I've always loved compliments. Giving them, receiving them. Not out of vanity, but because they bridge the space between people. A single kind word can land in the exact spot you didn't know was hungry for it. The world could use more of that, less critique, and more noticing what's good in each other. Later that evening, I wandered into a candlelit church under restoration where a Norwegian guitarist played a free concert under the full moon. His music filled the cavernous space like a prayer. I sat there, mesmerized. He was so talented.

Afterwards, I stumbled upon a gem of a restaurant and ordered the seafood risotto. I probably looked like a famished wolf as I inhaled it, but mid-bite, a fellow diner—an actual handsome Scandinavian road cyclist, still in his bib shorts and bike shoes—paused by my table.

"I just wanted to say," he said, "you are a very beautiful woman."

I was floored. I hadn't worn makeup in weeks. I hadn't even looked in a mirror, really. No styling, no filters, no effort—just me. With wild, untamed hair and unshaven body parts. Raw, real, and apparently radiant.

That night, I looked in the mirror. Barefaced, sun-warmed, and tired, I saw a woman who looked nothing like perfection but everything like herself. And somehow, that was more than enough. I gave myself a big, ear-to-ear smile.

Mum's Journal: No entry.

Maybe she was tired. Maybe she was having too much fun. Or maybe she had a day when words simply wouldn't do. Some days are meant to be felt, not recorded.

TINY PILGRIM TRUTH:

Beauty showed up when I stopped dressing it, painting it, and proving it. I felt it first; others simply recognized what was already there.

CHAPTER 21

SUPERMOONS, SADDLE HORSES, AND THE SACRED HALFWAY SEAT

September 18 – Day 17: Carrión to Moratinos (30 km)

I left Carrión under a blanket of darkness, guided only by the crunch of my boots and a spectacular pinkish supermoon that lit up the road like a runway for dreamers. It didn't just illuminate the path; it also whispered, "Yes, this way. Keep going." Birds offered a pre-dawn soundtrack, and for a time, it was just me, the Meseta, and their beautiful music.

A few hours in, I met the young Joanna from Poland. It was her first day on the Camino, and her emotional baggage clearly outnumbered her physical one. She was walking off a breakup, hoping the Camino would mend her heart and declutter her head. We walked and talked, and I think she found comfort in the companionship. As we stopped for coffee later, it turned out it was also her birthday, so I insisted we have a celebration with orange juice and croissants on me. She turned to me and said, "I'm so happy I ran into you today." There was real gratitude in her voice, and I felt something stir in me, something maternal, even protective. I saw a version of myself in her, and I was thrilled to be the steady presence I often needed at her age.

Then came the horses. Two Camino volunteers trotted up on horseback like knights in shining Gore-Tex. Being a horse lover (but sadly a horse allergy sufferer), I predictably threw caution to the wind and went full equine whisperer. Ten minutes of blissful snuggling later, I braced for the sneezing tsunami that, miraculously, never came. Of course, Camino horses have no allergy-producing dander; they know pilgrims already suffer enough.

It's one of life's great injustices: so many people who don't love horses get to be allergy-free, while I, who adore them with unhinged devotion, usually end up with hives, streaming eyes, and sneezing like I've been pepper-sprayed by joy.

The Meseta was generous that day: flat, golden, and under bluebird skies. It gifted me Jordan's voice in a surprise conversation that, as usual, made me happy. How do some people do that? Walk into your day and rewire your biochemistry? I wondered, was I that person enough for others?

Joanna, Ilze, and I were later joined by Beth from Wicklow. She was in her twenties and, as we'd say back home, a real live wire. For miles, we traded lighthearted tales of travel and late nights, laughter carrying us along. But eventually, her story shifted. Her mum, her best friend, had died of brain cancer in May. Out here, loss walks beside so many of us. It's sobering, yes, but also strangely connective.

We reached Moratinos, a blink-and-you'll-miss-it kind of town where Ilze and I ended up staying in the same Albergue. (There were only two, so not exactly serendipity).

Post-laundry and pilgrim scrub-down, we wandered into

what felt like a Wes Anderson outtake: a tiny, out-of-place wine bar serving up pinot and delight in equal measure. We toasted the day, the company, and the hope of many more laughs ahead.

On our way back, we climbed a hill and stumbled upon several bodegas, centuries-old wine cellars carved right into the earth like hobbit homes for Rioja lovers. At the top, we found two plain stone seats. Unassuming, unmarked, but sacred. These seats, it turns out, were our halfway point.

Halfway through something that was changing me. Yes, I was proud of the miles, but prouder that I was still open. Still walking. Still inside it. We finished the evening over pasta with a handful of other pilgrims, and I collapsed into bed, heavy with carbs and gratitude and slept like a log.

Mum's Journal

Left Carrión at 6 am with Peter. Pitch black. No moon. Amazing sky. Flat as far as the eye could see. Coffee in Ledigos—probably should've stayed, but got ambitious and kept climbing. Saw Carlos again (Belgian) and a Dutchman. Walked with Peter. Exhausted. The hostel in Terradillos was nice, but the people were horrid. No bed for Peter—he had to move on. I got the top bunk. Nice German roommate. French ones... less so. An actual fight broke out. Had a drink with Warren. Walked around. Village like death—so empty. Just an old man and some cats. Dinner was pleasant. Someone even asked about my morning plans.

Reading her words, I thought about a story she once told me about that very night. A cyclist arrived early and claimed a bed in the Albergue, even though Camino etiquette says walkers get priority before 5 p.m. He refused to give it up.

Mum, fluent in German and unbothered by confrontation, had a few well-chosen words with him. He moved.

She was like that: fierce when she needed to be. She had a strong voice and a deep sense of fairness and was never afraid to stand up for herself or for others. I knew I got that from her. I've always loved a good cause, always felt pulled to speak for the underdog. It's a trait that has served me well at times and, admittedly, made things harder in certain rooms. But out here, it made perfect sense. Courage belongs on the Camino.

TINY PILGRIM TRUTH:

What carries us forward isn't always muscle or will. Sometimes, it's the voice of a woman who once said, "Not today."

CHAPTER 22

MOON RISES, NAME BLANKS, AND BOLOGNESE MIRACLES

September 19 - Day 18: Moratinos to Bercianos (24km)

Another early solo start, and the Camino was on fire, literally. The moon was a massive orange orb setting behind me, while the pinks and purples of sunrise painted the sky. I was alone and loving it. Yesterday had been wonderfully social, but this morning was sacred solitude. Just 20 km ahead. I felt strong enough to double that, but reminded myself (again) that the Camino is not a marathon. Someone aptly called it "a slow dance with the divine."

In Sahagún, I rejoined Ilze and endured what I can confidently say was the worst croissant on the Camino. "Food is fuel," I told myself.

Sahagún itself was once one of the most important cities on the Camino Francés. Its Romanesque arches, Moorish-influenced churches, and medieval legacy whisper of its 11th-century glory, when it housed one of Spain's largest Benedictine monasteries. As we walked under one of its ancient entry arches, we also crossed from the province of Palencia into

Leon—a quiet milestone with big meaning. A new chapter begins.

We reached Bercianos, and I checked into a super chic hostel that doubled as a brewery. Arriving in my mind too early to start drinking beer, I grabbed a smoothie and sprawled on a sun-drenched chair, soaking in the vibes, the music, and the privilege of watching pilgrims wander by. "I'll Be Seeing You" played overhead, and my whole nervous system exhaled as I scribbled in my journal.

Later, I found myself sharing drinks with an ever-growing, delightfully ragtag Camino crew: Adrian from Yorkshire, Joanna, Gail, Tim, Chris, Olivier, Adam, and Lovina from India, who somehow talked me into a cigarette. It had been years. Truthfully, I enjoyed the nostalgia more than the smoke itself—a quick detour down memory lane. Luckily, I've always been blessed with a non-addictive streak, able to savor the moment for what it was while feeling grateful I'd left that habit behind twenty-five years ago.

At one point, in front of the group, Lovanya gave me some grief for forgetting her name. I'd only met her once in passing days earlier, but still, she wasn't wrong. Normally, I'm terrible with names, but I'd been doing a pretty incredible job this trip. I turned to her and said, "In my defense, I've walked over 300 miles and spoken to more people than I did in all of 2022. That said, your name is now officially tattooed on my brain." We both laughed. I never forgot her name after that, and I liked her a lot. She was real in the old way: slow to trust, didn't care if you liked her, and wouldn't fake liking you —not until she knew.

We were about three beers in when a very elderly man, bent like a comma under a giant pack, clacked into view. His name was Uwer, from Germany, 85 years old and absolutely wrecked. I called him over and handed him a beer. He downed it faster than I've seen anyone drink anything in my life. He didn't stay long, as he was probably worried his knees would seize up.

Ten minutes later, I noticed he'd left his poles behind.

Fueled by 3 pints of hops and a questionable sense of heroism, I declared, "I'm going after him!" and took off sprinting down the road like some Camino Avenger. It didn't take long to realize he had vanished. I returned, mildly winded and more than mildly defeated. The bartender, clearly inspired by my valiant, albeit failed, effort, offered to jump in her car to find him. She did. He was over the moon.

We all laughed, toasted again, and eventually collapsed into bed. I slept like I'd been tranquilized.

Mum's Journal

Walked alone. My foot was killing me yesterday, but loosened up after 2km. Saw a lovely hostel and coffee shop—wish I'd stayed. Got lost admiring a beautiful village. No footprints = wrong way. Lots of people lost today. Feeling very fit now. Walked into Sahagún and met a gorgeous Slovenian guy. Walked and sang with him. Forgot to check the signs—ended up in the wrong town. Found an old lady, woke up a taxi man. He brought me to the loveliest Albergue, and I shared a room with an Aussie girl. Felt like the G Hotel! Peter's bed was a literal shelf. A German lady and her daughter saw I was in bad shape and invited me to dinner. It was spaghetti Bolognese—my worst nightmare—and I scraped the plate clean!

I laughed out loud at Mum's Bolognese saga. For context: Mum had a fiercely limited palate. No melted cheese, no pasta, and certainly no sauce. She was famous for asking for a "dry plate" at restaurants, and waiters would blink, confused, until we clarified: no sauce at all. So the image of her happily devouring spaghetti Bolognese on the Camino? Absolute proof that this journey changes you. Maybe not your soul at first. But your taste buds? Absolutely.

TINY PILGRIM TRUTH:

Some transformations arrive in the form of "Bolognese" and a beer-fueled pole rescue. Either way, they count.

CHAPTER 23

NOTHER MAJOR IN MANSILLA MAYOR, SEPT. 21

September 20 – Day 19: Bercianos to Mansilla Mayor (26.7 km)

I woke up in a cozy little four-bed hostel, blessed by the rarest of Camino miracles: no snorers. I slipped out before sunrise, my headlamp slicing through the early mist as I set off solo. The sky was still holding its breath when I hit the trail—this is my favorite time of day, when the world hasn't quite woken up and it feels like it's just you, your breath, and the rhythm of your feet.

Today was mostly a solo act, but the Camino cast kept reappearing at pitstops like recurring characters in a feel-good miniseries: Adrian, Hette, Petra, Laura from Hungary, and, of course, Joann. We shared laughs and snacks, then drifted off in our own directions—some days are just meant for walking alone.

My stay tonight was a few kilometers beyond the typical stop, in a tiny hamlet boldly named Mansilla Mayor. I chuckled to myself as I walked through the town, thinking there was nothing "major" about the Mayor. With a population of 331 (and that's including livestock, I'm sure), it felt more like Mansilla Minor. But what it lacked in bustle, it made up for in blessed, glorious solitude. I had a private room. A private bath. A moment to exhale without having to recount my mileage, foot ailments, or evolving spiritual insights over dinner. As much as I enjoyed those gatherings and conversations, it was nice—actually essential for me—to have a break from them, too.

I had picked up pasta and sauce from a local shop earlier, but my rustic pension didn't offer a kitchen. So there I was, armed with uncooked carbs, two emergency cookies, and a rogue pear.

Mercifully, a tiny bar-restaurant emerged like an oasis and delivered salvation: one excellent burger and one cold beer. Dinner was sorted. Back in my room, I had a hot date with Mum's journal. I couldn't wait.

Mum's Journal

Left early with Peter and an Australian girl who quickly sped ahead. Rachelle, from Prince Edward Island, caught up —great craic walking with her. The route was barren but beautiful. We lunched roadside—no villages today. As always, the final 3 km were brutal. You start to question your life choices... and then you realize you have no other choice.

Queued outside the Albergue, I saw Carlos again and snagged a lower bunk (hallelujah). David, in short shorts, was in distress—his shorts had mysteriously vanished from the clothesline. He suspects theft. I can't stop laughing.

Later, I walked with Rachelle, still giggling over the "Great Camino Shorts Heist." We ran into Appalachian Al, aka Larry, aka "Snake," who had taken a shine to me. We had met before. He was charming, separated, and clearly looking for… something. He got a bit tipsy (rare out here) and propositioned me over dinner. I was tempted (he was good-looking), but his behavior was shabby. I walked back with him and declined politely. Peter also asked me to walk with him tomorrow to Leon. I slept like a baby.

Mum really did love men. She loved being adored, pursued, and bantered with, and honestly, she attracted attention the way the moon pulls tides. But her flirtation was equal opportunity too: waiters, women, babies, dogs. It wasn't about conquest; it was about connection. When she entered a room, the energy shifted, and what she drew out of people, she returned tenfold. She could light it up with a look or a laugh. That was her gift.

And tonight, in this tiny, quiet town that dared to call itself "Mayor," I feel her sparkle more than ever. In the stolen shorts saga. In the unexpected dinner invite. In the sense that, just like her, I have choices. Even when it feels like I don't.

TINY PILGRIM TRUTH:

You don't need to speak to shift a space. Walk in with calm, kindness, or joy and watch the air rearrange itself.

CHAPTER 24

LEON, LOSS, AND THE LESSONS WE CARRY

September 22- Day 20: Mansilla Mayor to Leon (20 km)

I woke up in Mansilla Mayor, quieter than a monastery during naptime, feeling surprisingly well-rested for someone who has walked halfway across Spain on foot. Today's walk to Leon was short, and I had a bit more spring in my step. But before lacing up, I had breakfast and a soul-deep conversation with Serena, a fellow pilgrim from the U.S. walking in memory of her only son, Austin, who died of a fentanyl overdose last year. Twenty-six. Gone in an instant. She shared that it felt like her world was over, and she was walking to convince herself otherwise.

Her quiet grace stayed with me all morning. It echoed a dear friend's story back home, and my heart ached for their loss, too. The Camino might be filled with sore feet and sunburns, but it's the invisible grief people carry that lingers longest. I walked today, holding that grief gently in my mental backpack, beside my gratitude.

What do we really need? Health. Family. Purpose. When I

stepped away from my corporate life, I thought I was chasing clarity or maybe just an exit ramp. But out here, stripped of all titles, agendas, and endless to-do lists, I feel oddly whole. Lighter. Anonymous, yes, but not erased. Just more... distilled.

The trail into Leon was kind, flat, sunlit, and dotted with familiar faces: Olivier, Joanna, Ilze. We shared snacks, small talk, and easy companionship. Olivier was charming and disarmingly good company. For a fleeting moment, I thought he'd make a fine match for Jordan, though this isn't the 1800s, and she hardly needs me casting suitors on the trail. Joanna, meanwhile, seemed to unfurl a little more each time I saw her, her sweetness and youthful eagerness and energy shining through as she leaned into the adventure. And Ilze, every meeting left me fonder. I'm not sure I've ever met a Dutch person I didn't like; there's a disarming practicality and candor to them that I find utterly charming.

Leon itself is a marvel—a feast for the senses and a balm for the soul. Once the capital of the ancient Kingdom of Leon, this city has played host to kings, crusaders, and now—us: pilgrims with questionable hygiene and hopeful hearts. We entered through the Arco de la Cárcel and wandered into streets that felt as if they were whispering old secrets.

We had splurged on a "superbly central" hostel, which turned out to be code for "surrounded by noise and suspicious bathroom residue." There's something about stranger hairs in shared showers that never gets easier. Enlightenment, it seems, has a texture. And sometimes that texture is... wiry.

Later, we strolled up the street to visit the Cathedral, La Pulchra Leonina, a Gothic masterpiece built in a miraculous 50 years. With nearly 2,000 square meters of stained glass, it doesn't just let in light; it sets it loose. I stood beneath its technicolor glow and did what I always do in every church since losing Gran and now Mum: I lit two candles. I watched the tiny flames flicker with big feelings surging.

That evening, Ilze and I joined Tim, Joanna, and Olivier for several generous glasses of Rioja, the kind that makes hours slip by unnoticed. Tim's pockets proved even bigger than his heart, which was no small feat, and it was nearly impossible to reach the bar before he did. He was walking the Camino in memory of his father, raising money for heart disease research. He was the kind of person who collected friends effortlessly, scattering them across the world with no sense of quota or limit. Later, a dinner reservation for six morphed into twelve, nearly sending our waiter into an existential crisis. The food was good, and the bill-splitting theatrics were comical. Later that night, I opened Mum's journal. She, too, had reached Leon.

Mum's Journal

Up early. Leave with Rachelle. No sign of Peter or Snake. Enjoy the route, a little hilly, mostly near roads, but very nice. Met Carlos on the way out of Mansilla. He's so friendly, always stops to say hello, but has no English. Last 5km to Leon through a very industrial area, but ok, and we had great fun anyway. Met Peter for coffee. At Leon, a welcome table is set up just before the bridge to show us the route in. How wonderful. Lots more walking. Get to the Albergue and there were a lot of people queuing in the Archway of the Benedictine Monastery.

I met a hippy-type girl with a 1-year-old baby tied to her front and her 13-year-old, less-than-enthusiastic son. He hates walking, he tells me. She tells Rachelle it is difficult for her (she's English) as people seem to be judging her. God, I think, no wonder. Hostels are no place for babies. And the son does the minding while she showers, etc. Not much fun for him. We never met them again. Go out for lunch and a walk, and Rachelle goes shopping. I met Carlos for coffee in a square near the hostel. Also met Warren for a drink, and were joined by Al and Peter, and discovered they had left earlier in the morning as Al had a medical problem and needed to get to Leon early. Rachelle joins, and we all have dinner. Had a drink later with Rachelle in the lovely square in front of the Albergue. Carlos joined us, and I introduced him to Rachelle. I was tired, left early. I am in a bunk beside baby, dreading night feeds. Sleep like a log, heard nothing.

Mum had the conviction of a High Court judge and the flexibility of a cast-iron skillet. Once she formed an opinion, whether it was about people, politics, or pasta, it was more or less set in concrete. She could size someone up in ten seconds flat, assign them a verdict, and mentally shelve them under a tidy label.

And yet, she was insatiably curious. She devoured books on Irish history, Gandhi, Nehru, and Churchill, and her appetite for knowledge was vast. But her curiosity had limits —guardrails. Certain subjects or people were just outside the syllabus.

That night, it made me wonder: had I inherited the same tendencies? I was absolutely different in the sense of being the consummate generalist. Too many things interested me. I was curious about everything. But what about hasty judgment? How often had I boxed people in before they had the chance to unfold? Guilty as charged.

Leon reminded me that awe and ache can live in the same

breath, that we can be both weary and wonderstruck, and that sometimes, the best way to honor the losses we carry is to keep walking—with fewer assumptions and more space in our hearts for the complexity of it all.

TINY PILGRIM TRUTH:

The real weight of the Camino isn't in your pack. It's in what you're willing to unpack. About others. About yourself.

CHAPTER 25

DETOURS, DIGESTIFS, AND A HIGHWAY THROUGH SUNFLOWERS

September 2 - Day 21: Leon to San Martín via the scenic route. (34 km)

Woke up at 7 a.m. feeling like I'd barely closed my eyes thanks to a cocktail of bunk bed mayhem, street revelers, and one enthusiastic snorer who sounded like he was power-washing gravel in his sleep. Still, I decided to skip the more direct route to Villadangos and instead take the rural road to San Martín via Villar de Mazarife for two reasons. One, it was the more scenic and soul-soothing option, and two, because Mum walked that exact path, and I didn't want to miss a single step she took.

The detour meant adding 14 km to an already decent trek, but my legs felt like steel and my heart felt light. Ilze joined me, my ever-more-beloved Camino companion. We walk with that rare kind of flow: silence without awkwardness, conversation without filler. Our chats jump from the profound to the ridiculous, often with a side of hilariously inappropriate humor.

Ilze shared that she chose this route because her late boyfriend, Charles, had walked it years ago. He died just two months earlier. Her grief was so present but so gracefully carried; it reminded me again how this walk is less about the destination and more about honoring the ones who walked before us.

We stopped for lunch, digging into a dreamy chicken paella, while Ilze nobly settled for a tomato salad that she absolutely did not enjoy as much as she pretended to. I offered her a bite of mine. She declined. I admired her restraint and mourned her missed mouthful.

The last 10 km was straight out of a painting. Ten-foot sunflower fields stretched like golden sentinels on either side of a narrow dirt road. It felt like the Camino had parted the sunflowers just for us, creating a quiet, sacred highway to somewhere better. Magic. Real magic. It truly did feel like heaven.

When we finally rolled into San Martín, barely a town and more a few sparse homes across a junction, we headed to our separate hostels. I showered, grabbed a cold beer, and signed up for the 7 p.m. communal dinner like a seasoned pilgrim pro. I called Neil and the kids, who, I was both proud and mildly offended to report, were thriving without me.

Dinner was a riot. Ilze joined in, along with Sandy from Canada, Steve from New Jersey, and best friends Amy and Lisa from the States. Too many after-dinner digestifs were consumed. Too many belly laughs to count. And I slept like a drunken saint, flat out for nine glorious hours. Apparently, laughs and digestifs are the ultimate sleep-aid duo.

Mum's Journal

½ a cup of coffee and bread for breakfast. Leave really

early with Rachelle. Immediately take the wrong turn. Much walking around Leon. No hope!! Then see the bus and the bus driver points to the route. Wrong turn twice and so much walking. Beautiful route. So quiet and so peaceful. Stop at quaint village: Fresno del Camino, for breakfast. Must wait for bread delivery. Sit out in the sun and wait with many cats!!! Van pulls up with the guy to deliver the bags of baguettes. Great fun today. Mazarife is so old and cute. On the outskirts I see the new hostel with flowers and sun chairs. Book bed, breakfast and dinner. So clean. Walk around the village and meet two elderly ladies and took some pictures for them. Met Peter and Salvadore, a beautiful, friendly Italian, for lunch. He is magnificent and has a certain spirituality about him. Have dinner in the hostel, best meal for ages, to die for. All nationalities at a very long table. Sleep like a log. The next morning, I have the best breakfast ever there, elderly smiling chef. Didn't meet any of the usual crowd. Choice of paths and destinations today.

As I read Mum's words, her getting lost, then found, then lost again, I wondered. How often did she lose her way in life, without even realizing it? And how many of us do the same? Do we always know we've wandered off the path, or do we need the right signpost or maybe the right person to steer us gently back?

Mum got so many of the big things right: a career she loved, five children who adored her, and a community of friends who lit up in her presence. But I think she longed, more than anything, for that epic, sweep-you-off-your-feet kind of love. And maybe she thought she'd found it until she realized, too late, that she had veered off course.

And maybe that's the quiet heartbreak of it all: not the

path we take, but the moment we realize it isn't leading where we thought.

Still, she walked. And so do I. Onward.

TINY PILGRIM TRUTH:

Not all wrong turns are mistakes. Some just take the long way to the right place.

CHAPTER 26

JESUS SANDALS & JOUSTING KNIGHTS

September 23 - Day 22: San Martín to Astorga (24 km)

I set out alone again in the dark, a ritual I've grown strangely fond of. There's something sacred about slipping into the day before it begins, as if borrowing time from the world before it wakes. The quiet, the cool air, the rhythm of my steps—it's a meditation.

The early stretch to Hospital de Órbigo was smooth and scenic, and there, like clockwork, I ran into Ilze. Over coffee and a croissant, we fell back into our well-worn rhythm of deep chats and laughs.

A few miles in, we stumbled on one of the most beautiful bridges I had ever seen. The Puente de Órbigo, a medieval marvel stretching across the Río Órbigo, was like something out of a chivalric fever dream. Built in the 13th century on the bones of an older Roman bridge, it boasts over 20 arches and an even more dramatic backstory. In 1434, a knight named Suero de Quiñones held the bridge for 30 days, jousting any poor soul who dared cross it, all to prove his love to a woman who didn't return it. Ah, unrequited love.

Past the bridge, we climbed a hill and came across a barefoot man in the ruins who had laid out fruit, juice, and nuts on makeshift market tables. No prices, just a "donativo." I grabbed a banana, some walnuts, and orange juice that tasted like sunshine. I bumped into Ed again and his cheerful friends from Ireland, who had joined him for a week. How nice to have friends join you on a section of the walk, I thought. This didn't change the fact that I was very glad to be walking the Camino alone. This walk, I was increasingly realizing, was something I needed to do on my own.

As I walked, I was congratulating myself on how miraculously responsible I'd been. Nothing lost since Burgos, and that guidebook hardly counted since it had eventually found its way back to me. Naturally, the very act of thinking this was the universe's cue to remind me otherwise. My backpack felt suspiciously lighter. Heart thumping, I yanked it off and tore it open. Empty space where salvation should be. My shoes, my blister-banishing, soul saving miracles of modern engineering, were gone. Fifteen kilometers behind me. The mind reeled. Do I retrace my steps for my beloved Tevas, or keep walking in my sneakers and trust they'll see me through to Santiago?

First things first: I called the hostel where, sadly but understandably, the manager had no English. Just as I fumbled with Google Translate, divine timing swept in, wearing a police badge. A local officer visiting the hostel took the phone, her English calm and flawless. "I'll drive them to you," she said, as if chauffeuring abandoned pilgrim footwear was part of the standard policing manual. I began to sputter some noble protest about walking back myself, but she cut me off with a crisp, "It's only ten minutes by car." Ten minutes! After I had huffed and puffed for hours across sun-baked terrain. My earlier groaning about the impossible tragedy of retracing my steps suddenly felt... a touch theatrical. Gratitude, however, was immediate and overwhelming.

Shoes reunited and dignity (mostly) restored, I limped triumphantly into Astorga by early afternoon and was smitten almost instantly. A former Roman outpost turned chocolate capital? I was a self-proclaimed chocolate addict, so this was a match made in heaven. Honestly, why bother walking all the way to Santiago when the promised land was clearly here, dipped in cocoa? Naturally, the universe caught wind of my heretical thoughts and intervened: the famed chocolate factory was closed on Mondays. Now, I'm no religious stickler, but isn't the Lord's Day of Rest supposed to be Sunday? And really, if ever there were a day humanity needed chocolate, surely it's Monday. Thankfully, the town's shops were well-stocked, and I undertook the noble task of cultural enrichment by sampling my way through the plaza, square by square, truffle by truffle.

I wandered through the Episcopal Palace, Gaudí's stone dreamscape, and stood beneath the towering cathedral beside it, both rising like ancient sentinels guarding the sacred and the forgotten. They stopped me in my tracks. To think Gaudí gave the world these impossible buildings, carved from vision, madness, and genius—what a legacy.

And then I wondered, "What am I building? Will anything I've made outlast me? Will my life echo, or will it evaporate the moment I stop breathing?" Permanence isn't always set in stone. Sometimes, it's in the people you shape, the stories you tell, and the love you dare to give away.

That night, I had my first curry dinner on the Camino and lively conversations with fellow pilgrims back at the hostel. I crawled into bed and passed out like a well-fed toddler. Eight blissful hours of horizontal, dreamless sleep followed.

Mum's Journal

Beautiful breakfast, gorgeous chef. Left in the dark with Rachelle, but walked mostly alone. It was a lovely stage. Beautiful views to Astorga from the hill, 6 km out at Anto Santo Toribio. I found it tough going and hot and steep in parts. 4 km out, I stopped at an old ruin where a young guy has been camping for a year or two. He has set up a pay-if-you-want stall. So glad I took orange juice. The rest of the walk to Astorga was too difficult, almost unbearable, especially climbing over the railway ramps. A steep, steep climb up to the hostel, into which I nearly collapsed. Shivering in the bunk, Salvadore talks me back to normal. He is such a beautiful human. I recover, shower, and go for coffee. It's a lovely town with old buildings. Dinner with Al, Rachelle, Peter, and Tristan—a lovely mid-40s Arizonian, red-headed guy—very friendly and good-humored. I'm sleeping so well.

I picture us both, years apart, sipping orange juice from the same hilltop stall, served by the same barefoot man. He's been there at least twelve years, bridging time and stories. I think of Mum at 68, doing this walk eighteen years older than I am now. What kind of shape will I be in then? Will I still be walking forward?

She was my blueprint: glamorous, charming, whip-smart, hilariously judgmental, and filled with a kind of turbocharged energy that made everyone feel ten feet tall. I spent so much of my life wanting to be just like her. But as I grew older, I saw the cracks, the complexities, the demons. She wasn't perfect; she was human. Aren't we all?

And honestly? That's the greatest thing she could've been. Because if I can inherit even half her spark and learn to carry it with my own light… then, as she would say, "Andy darling, you'll be off to the races."

TINY PILGRIM TRUTH:

There's a quiet courage in letting someone help you. Grace lives in that space—between your pride and their kindness.

CHAPTER 27

AMBIVERTS, ALTITUDES, AND AWKWARD UNDERWEAR ENCOUNTERS

September 24 - Day 23: Astorga to Foncebadón (25 km)

Another early departure, another day that begins before the sun does. I'm deep into this rhythm now with this almost monastic ritual of waking, walking, and wondering. The air is cool, dry, and tinged with mountain promise. Today, we start the climb, both literally and metaphorically. Tomorrow, I'll reach the highest physical point on the Camino.

The flatlands give way to forest. The greens grow richer, the air heavier, and the trees begin to thicken around me like a divine cocoon. It's as if the landscape itself is rising to meet whatever I'm becoming.

I met up with Ruth, Robyn, and Tim over a long, lazy lunch, which was so much fun. I decided to stretch today's walk further. Instead of stopping in Rabanal, I pressed on to Foncebadón, a crumbling hilltop village that feels like the edge of the world. I want to make it to the "Cruz de Ferro" at sunrise tomorrow.

The scenery on the way up? Pure magic. Hills undulate like slow waves, clouds sink into valleys, and everything feels hushed and holy.

We finally roll into Foncebadón, equal parts charming and haunted, and collapse joyfully into a stone-walled tavern called "La Taberna de Gaia," which may or may not have doubled as a medieval dungeon in a past life. But with no museums, cathedrals, or hills left to climb, we had no choice but to hit the cave-pub. From the street, it looked like nothing more than a cramped little hut, but inside, a staircase plunged into the vast cellar of the bar.

A few beers too many later, back at our hostel, we were singing along to an Argentinian pilgrim's guitar like it was "Camino Karaoke" night. I walked the more-than-slightly inebriated Robyn back to her hostel (all of 20 feet away), waved goodnight to Ed and his crew, whom I caught a glimpse of at the hostel next door, and headed back to my own bunk.

And then... the night takes a turn.

Let's just say my hostel roommate situation was "eccentric with a hint of potential Dateline episode." A curious Englishman, who had casually mentioned over dinner that he was an ex-con, was also, unfortunately, my bunkmate. He gave me the kind of prolonged eye contact that makes you instinctively inventory exits. Tim, gallant and ever the saint, offered to swap beds with me. I declined, as I felt ten people in the room felt safe enough.

Until it didn't.

Around 2 a.m., I woke to find said ex-convict pacing the room in his tighty-whities. Then, in one smooth and unprovoked motion, he delivered a swift kick to Tim (who, in fairness, was snoring like a leaf blower), turned on white noise at aircraft volume, and tucked himself back in like this was simply how civilized people wind down. I spent the rest of the night lying stiffly on my side, religiously facing the wall and hoping this Camino lesson didn't involve self-defense or small claims court.

Sleep was, understandably, brief.

Mum's Journal

Set off early with Peter, Rachelle, and Tristan. Best fun of the Camino. Coffee stop every 5 km. Heading towards the mountains, so the last bit was tiring. We reached Rabinal, and Rachelle thinks we have 3 km to go. No—this cute little village is Rabinal, and we found a gorgeous private voluntary Albergue beside the church. So cute and very nice people. Had lunch with Tristan and Rachelle. Such a fab company. I sat alone in the afternoon in the wild garden behind the hostel. I eat beans in the hostel as there is no time for dinner. There is an ancient church that is magnificent, just by the hostel. I have a drink in the bar with Rachelle and meet Chris Lindt, a Tipperary farmer. It's such fun, and I get great sleep.

Mum had the rare ability to be the life of the party and totally at peace in her own company. Like Mum, I've always been an ambivert, as alive in the sparkle of company as in the quiet of my own thoughts. Equally at home in conversation or in silence, we were very much alike. Reading her words tonight, I smiled. "Coffee every 5 km. Laughter. Beans for dinner. A flirty chat with a farmer from Tipp." She really was so happy on this adventure.

TINY PILGRIM TRUTH:

The strangest nights can make for the best stories, especially the ones you swear you never want to repeat.

CHAPTER 28

LEAVING STONES, GATHERING STORIES

September 25 - Day 24: Foncebadón to Molinaseca (20 km)

After a night of sleep that was more haunted house than hilltop haven, I woke early, determined to make it to the Cruz de Ferro by sunrise. After a slice of toast and a solid black coffee, I was joined by my fellow pilgrims: Tim, hilariously hardy for such an early hour, and Ruth, as usual, socially energetic. The mist hugged the cottages as we set off, the air cool and heavy with the scent of damp earth. Cows mooed, roosters crowed, and the birds sang a morning anthem. Despite the pitch black, it all felt reassuringly alive.

We reached the Cruz de Ferro just before dawn; the world was still cloaked in fog and silence. At first, we nearly missed it. The cross was barely visible at dusk, a thin wooden silhouette perched on its iron pole above a mountain of stones left by centuries of pilgrims. The sun began to inch over the horizon, bleeding light into the mist, and the place felt almost otherworldly, suspended between night and day, burden and release. Tradition holds that each pilgrim carries a stone from home, a weight of sorrow, forgiveness, or hope. In that hushed, liminal moment, I climbed the mound, stones in hand, ready to lay mine down.

Of course, I couldn't leave just one stone, so I left three. The first, for those I've loved and lost. The second, for the pieces of myself I'm ready to release—control, ego, impatience—though Jordan, ever helpful, offered to provide a longer list if I found myself short on flaws. And the third, the largest of them all, was for Mum.

I wished her peace on this cruel, unchosen journey with Alzheimer's. And for me, peace in letting go of the Mum I used to have, so I could better love the Mum I still have. The tears came, slow and steady.

Soon, familiar faces gathered. Hetty, Ilze, Olivier, Adam, Paulina, and I watched the sunrise spill gold over the mountains. We snapped a photo, less about the scenery and more about an unspoken pact that this mattered. True to my Irish roots, I perfected the art of the elegant vanish, slipping quietly into the morning haze before the sun got too cheeky and blew my cover. This was definitely a day I wanted to walk alone.

The descent was spectacular, Galicia revealing itself like a flirtatious hostess: wild heather, sharp hills, valleys filled with cloud. It reminded me of the Scottish glens we visited as a family last summer—melancholic, majestic, and ancient.

I paused in the quaint village of Acebo for coffee and a slice of lemon cake fresh from the oven. Recharged, I practically galloped goat-like into Molinaseca, a gem of a town nestled by a river and crossed by an impeccable Roman bridge that has stood its ground since the first century. The town, whose name derives from "Molino" (mill), was historically a milling hub for pilgrims and locals alike. Today it feels like a movie set—a cluster of stone houses, narrow streets, and the gentle hum of river water underneath.

I checked into "The Way" Hostel, perched right on the river. Showered and starving, I found a restaurant on the bank and ordered pizza and beer. That's when I noticed Tim, an impeccably dressed elderly man, vintage in the best sense. I invited him to join me, and what a conversation that sparked.

Tim was 80. He'd first done the Camino a decade ago with his sister, who was grieving the death of her daughter. Alone much of the way, Tim had a transformative experience and, upon returning to his corporate empire in the U.S., sold his four companies. He packed up and moved to Molinaseca, planning to buy a church—proof that Americans will try to purchase just about anything, fueled by that unshakable optimism that everything has a price tag. Instead, he became a steward of the 17th-century Church of Saint Nicolas, hosting pilgrim gatherings each week.

We spoke of life's second chapters, of not waiting for grief to push us into living more fully. He made me think: How will I bring the Camino home? Not as a story, but as a new way of being.

Later, I snagged a massage from Lucy, the fruit-stand woman from just outside town. She even drove me to Ponferrada for an ATM, narrating the region's history with pride, only on the Camino.

Ilze and I capped the night by visiting the church, which Tim graciously opened for us, lighting it by candlelight and giving us a tour that felt timeless.

As I tucked into bed, I wondered if things were becoming more eventful or if I was just more awake to life now.

I reached for Mum's journal.

Mum's Journal

Left alone in the dark. One kilometer out, wrong path. German girls call me back. I call ahead to the German man in front of me—he is lost too. Two kilometers out, it starts to rain. I'm on the mountain now, with strong winds, and quite a few people. I stop at Foncebadon for a coffee. I meet Antonia, and we chat in our own languages. I meet her in most places; she always stops for a bit and has no English. I think I have eleven words of Spanish now. Off I go. It's like Ireland, the wildest of Connemara in the worst winter weather.

I stop at Acebo, 17 km, for coffee. I am frozen. I meet Chris. As I leave, Tristan tells me there is one bed left. I really want to stay, but I need to go 10 km more, so I say goodbye. It's a very steep downhill, so I stop and take a break for a while. It's very pretty. Today was the highest point on the Camino at 1,505 meters. It felt like it.

I was very tired coming into Molineseca. I met Rachelle having lunch in an outside café, and when Chris arrived, he looked so sharp and cool (not fair). I made off for the hostel priv that Rachelle had booked. It's very nice. I booked breakfast for the next morning. I had dinner in a lovely place with Rachelle and Chris, and it was loads of fun. I am in the next bunk to Chris and almost don't mind. A year ago, I didn't know what a hostel looked like and had no desire to find out.

I laughed at our mutual linguistic floundering. Our Spanish was capped at about eleven words each. I'd tried the Duolingo app, but my French love affair got in the way. Maybe next time, I'll start the Camino from Paris and get the best of both worlds.

What really struck me, though, was that Mum never mentioned the Cruz de Ferro. This was such a significant stage and relic of the Camino. Not a word. Did she leave a stone? Did she even pause? She was a documenter of facts, not feelings. Her journals are rich with people and places, but almost no interior world. Maybe she was too exhausted to introspect. Perhaps the purpose of her journal wasn't reflection, but record-keeping—the names, faces, and places of what she coined "the greatest adventure of her life." A way to capture memories before they slipped away. Maybe she was already aware her memory was beginning to betray her, and how terrifying that must have been for someone who prized her intellect and wit so fiercely. She had joked, more than once, about never wanting to become "the village idiot," and perhaps that fear had already taken root.

Her entries read like telegraphs: succinct, punchy, often hilarious, but rarely vulnerable. I used to joke that her emails read like old-school telegraphs and that she was being charged by the word. She laughed hard at that.

I miss that laugh. But tonight, I feel closer to her, not just through her words but through the silences between them.

And maybe that's the real lesson of the Cruz de Ferro: not just what you leave behind, but what you finally understand you have been carrying all along.

TINY PILGRIM TRUTH:

Some burdens aren't lifted by effort but by honesty. The moment you name them, they begin to weigh less.

CHAPTER 29

RAIN, RESILIENCE, AND THE ROAD TO VILLAFRANCA

September 26 - Day 25: Molinaseca to Villafranca (30 km)

I set out in the dark under a torrential downpour that showed no signs of relenting. But with my trusty poncho and well-worn Tevo sandals, I embraced the rain with a stoic "dry-ish" optimism. As Mum always said, "The gear is everything." She wasn't wrong.

Ilze soon joined me, and together we trudged like drowned rats to the ancient town of Ponferrada, where a bowl of oatmeal with raspberries and walnuts awaited me like a culinary hug from the Camino gods. It was perfect—nourishing, warm, and suspiciously tailored to my tastes. The Camino provides.

We passed the majestic Templar Castle, a 10th-century fortress that looks like it was plucked straight from a medieval fantasy. The Knights Templar, equal parts monk and warrior, held these lands with a mysterious grip, protecting pilgrims with swords in one hand and scripture in the other. Their shadowy legacy has inspired everything from conspiracy theories to "The Da Vinci Code." Passing by their towering stronghold, I half-expected a cloaked knight to gallop past. I was enthralled by this period.

I checked Mum's journal that morning and noted she'd stopped in Cacabelos, not making it to Villafranca. In homage, I stopped there for lunch and devoured the Galician specialty of pulpo (octopus) with potatoes. Delicious, but far too much for one pilgrim with more miles to go.

By the time we crossed yet another glorious bridge into Villafranca del Bierzo, the rain had surrendered. Villafranca, founded in the 11th century, is often called the "little Compostela" because pilgrims too weary or ill to continue could receive a similar blessing here as in Santiago. The town, framed by medieval streets and nestled among lush vineyards, whispered of history and grace.

I checked into a charming boutique hotel, complete with pressed white sheets and a bathtub that was practically a spiritual experience. After a revitalizing soak, I strolled through the town, visiting the Santa Maria Church and Museum, and capped the evening with a pilgrim's mass, where I spotted several familiar faces. As fate would have it, I stumbled into a bar where Tim, Olivier, Adam, and Paulina were holding court, so I bought a round. It was a fun, unexpected night that ended with the best sleep I'd had in days.

Mum's Journal

Breakfast in Albergue. Left early with Rachelle. Beautiful walk into Ponferrada, cute village, chickens coming to life—no people as it is too early. Then I lost my way in Ponferrada. Walked about 10 km on the road—busy and boring. Stopped at Camponaraya and met Kevin, a nurse from Australia, and another man who had also lost his way. He was quite rude, and we could only laugh over our late breakfast. He looked so miserable and seemed to resent our good humor. Walked on. Lovely but very tiring.

Coming into Cacabelos, I felt it was too much. I saw a sign for the hotel, so I went in. Bliss. A three-way shower. Rachelle had been 100 yards ahead, so I couldn't yell at her that I was stopping. I ate alone. I met Carlos and later Salvador. Now I see why it's more fun to stay in hostels. It's like a meeting of pals. You don't feel alone even when you are. But it's nice to spread myself and my meager clothes a bit. I slept okay.

Mum had an uncanny ability to find humor in nearly everything—except perhaps her marriage and divorce. Like many Irish women of her generation, she had little patience for wallowing. Her mantra was simple: "You've two arms and two legs, so get on with it." As a child, I found that maddening when all I wanted was a dose of empathy, but now I see it as a pillar of resilience and optimism that runs in my veins.

That said, I've worked on trying to make space for moments of vulnerability for myself and my kids. It's okay to sit with sadness or frustration, but only for a time. Then, back up we get. We're made of solid stuff.

I glanced at my Camino guidebook. 700 km walked, just 187 km and 9 days to go. The end loomed, but was I ready? Had I found what I needed, left what I should? Not yet, I thought. But in true Mum fashion, I reminded myself: I'll get there. And when I do, I'll be ready.

TINY PILGRIM TRUTH:

"Walk long enough without luxury, and you'll weep over hot water, clean sheets, and a door that locks. That's the gift of absence: it rewires what matters."

CHAPTER 30

RIVERS, REVELRY, AND RAIN

September 27 - Day 26: Villafranca to Las Herrerías (22 km)

I set off in the dark under yet another relentless downpour. Despite the soggy forecast, I took my time, punctuating the trek with frequent coffee stops and snacks because, why suffer when there are caffeine and carbs abound?

Somewhere along the descent, a gorgeous river called to me like a siren. I scrambled down to sit by its side for twenty minutes, watching my rain-soaked toes peep from under my poncho, the river rippling in the background. Pure, ridiculous joy. Who knew a damp sit-down could feel like a spa retreat?

The day's official endpoint was O Cebreiro, but I decided I'd had enough of the rain for one day and stopped a few kilometers earlier in Las Herrerías, a quaint farming village with an irresistible hostel. The place had rustic charm and a lively bar-restaurant vibe. Sure, the restaurant staff were also the check-in crew, and yes, my food took ages, but I was in no rush, not when the walls oozed warmth and wine.

I checked in, made up my bunk with the tissue-paper-thin

under-sheet provided (classic), showered, and returned to the bustling restaurant. There, I met Ilia, a lovely Ukrainian woman in her 30s, mother of two young children, walking a week of the Camino before her husband joined her for the last few days. Sensing her nerves about the mountainous terrain ahead, I offered to walk with her the next day. She looked relieved and delighted.

As she left, I caught some loud Northern Irish accents from the table next to me. An elderly couple and a younger man (my age, thank you very much) invited me to join them. That's all it takes out here: a familiar accent, and you're family.

Tom and Mary were in Villafranca celebrating Mary's 70th birthday because, as they proudly declared, "the Camino is the world's longest pub crawl." That should have been my cue to exit, but alas, I stayed. The gin and tonics flowed (I left more behind than I drank), the conversation slurred, and before long, it was evident that the birthday lady needed to call it a night—and needed help doing so.

Tom (who was also in bad shape) and I managed to get her up, but not without the help of a kind local. The nephew was as useful as a waterproof teabag. We carried her, quite literally, to her bed, depositing her with as much dignity as we could muster.

As I stepped outside for air and my own graceful exit, the nephew, still loitering, decided to seize the moment. "Fancy coming back to my hostel for a drink?" he asked with a devilish grin.

"Ah, yes. Nothing gets me in the mood like carrying your drunk aunt to bed. Sadly, I'm fresh out of bad decisions tonight."

He blinked, stunned. I smiled sweetly, turned on my heel, and went to bed, unimpressed but mildly entertained.

A pretty ghastly night of little sleep followed. A room of ten snoring, shuffling pilgrims does that to you. The hostel life was starting to wear thin.

Mum's Journal

Cacabelos to Ruitelán

Up early, very dark. Cold and windy. The weather changed yesterday evening. Strange leaving the quiet hotel with no walkers about. 1km out, meet a lovely, quiet Norwegian man. He stops at 1st coffee shop and I push on. Love every moment, the undulating hills are beautiful even in the darkness. Carlos, Eric and Ed catch up, and we walk together. They are flying, so I tell them to go ahead. It starts to rain fairly heavily, but I plod on.

Meet Carlos and the gang, having a mixed-language, difficult discussion. Eric is very upset as he has just discovered he left his towel behind at the hostel and wants to go back for it. Carlos is laughing, calling him a "big baby." It's 4 km back, which would be an extra 8 km for the poor chap. Eric is German, so I talk to him in my rusty German. Apparently, it's not just a towel; it's bigger than normal. I say, "Buy another." Carlos wins. It seems to be of great value to Eric (maybe from some girl), so Carlos says he will call the hostel and ask them to send it ahead. All good, and we march off laughing in the pouring rain.

A gang, led by Antonia, is spotted way below us outside the Albergue in Villafranca and roars a big welcome. In the village, Carlos buys us a big breakfast. I leave separately; I don't wait. It's a hard route, and I have decided to catch up with Rachelle by walking the extra distance. Up and up and up the hill I go. Five hours in the rain. Exhausted and no longer able to continue, I make it to Ruitelán, a tiny village. I can't speak when I arrive at the equally tiny Albergue, so they give me a glass of wine. Up to the loft I go. Cold, miserable. A group dinner, pasta—I instinctively contract and then devour. A beautiful soup. Coffee, wine, bed, and sleep. I miss the fun people.

I loved reading Mum's entry and seeing how we shared the same grim weather. Her stamina and her sheer determination to push on floored me. That relentless uphill, in those conditions, at her age?

She had her tribe now, as I was beginning to have mine. The Camino reflects life: some relationships are fleeting, others enduring. Some people are there for a laugh, some to teach you a lesson, and some are the type that will help you reunite with that towel, no matter how ridiculous it seems.

I realized I was leaning into the social side of the Camino, saying yes more often and being more open to connection. Mum was right; it's more fun that way.

As I glanced at my Camino guidebook, 700 km walked, 165 km to go. The end was looming, and I was equally excited and dreading it.

TINY PILGRIM TRUTH:

There's a strange joy in helping someone into bed, dodging bad decisions, and realizing that, somehow, you're the adult now.

CHAPTER 31

LIFE, DEATH, AND A FULL BOTTLE OF RIOJA

September 28 - Day 27: Herrerías to Triacastela (30 km)

They say the Camino gives you what you need, not what you want. On Day 27, it gave me thick clouds to climb through, a bottle of wine I didn't ask for, and a reminder, gentle and jarring—that life can shift in a breath.

We left Herrerías shrouded in mist, the kind that feels enchanted one minute and foreboding the next. Ilia, my new Ukrainian walking companion, and I powered up the steep wooded ascent to La Faba, croissant-fueled and poncho-clad. The trail wound past sleepy cows, curious horses, and enormous dogs lounging like furry gatekeepers of the mountain. It felt as if I were walking through a folktale.

By midday, the clouds parted, revealing the vast, lush drama of Galicia. At the mountaintop village of O Cebreiro, we met the usual suspects—Tim, Ruth, Adam, Olivier, and Ed—for lunch at a windswept roadside café. The menu boasted a three-course meal for 11 euros, with wine. I assumed we'd share a bottle. But no, each of us was handed a full bottle, as if we were being dared to prove our worth in Rioja. This wasn't lunch; this was quite definitely a situation.

After lunch, a bunch of us started the lovely long walk down the mountain. It was turning out to be quite possibly the most enjoyable walk of the Camino.

And then the day turned.

My phone rang. Ilze, still up on the mountain, sounded shaken. A 59-year-old Danish pilgrim, whom I'd seen with his friend the night before in the hostel, had collapsed not long after leaving the same lunch spot. He had suffered a sudden and fatal heart attack. He died before emergency services could arrive. Ilze, Lovanya, Joanna, and Olivier stayed with him until the end, for three hours, offering comfort to his friend, Ole, as best they could.

The weight of that news sat with me for the rest of the day —a sharp reminder of how quickly things can shift, even in sunlight. And then, as if the Camino needed to rebalance the scale between heartbreak and farce, I heard that Ed, still full of wine and optimism, had followed his GPS straight into a cemetery, two miles off course after an already brutal walk.

That night, back in a rickety bunk in a forgettable hostel in Triacastela, the day's events hit me like a late-arriving wave. I cried. Not just for Ole's friend and his family, for Ole, but for Mum. His sudden ending mirrored the slow, merciless unraveling of her memory. I missed her—the razor-sharp wit, the irreverence, and her advice.

I scribbled thoughts into my notebook. Coffee, wine, scribbles: my new survival strategy. The mix of absurdity and aching had become strangely familiar.

Mum's Journal

First out the door in the darkness through the tiny village.

Off road over the bridge, pass fields, woods and another deserted village. Thank God (or Ben) for my little light. Very determined now to make the distance, 30km. About 2 pm, I see a coffee shop open and inside met a lovely couple, Michael was in the army (aged 26) from Winterthur. His plan is to do the last 100km into Santiago in a day (maybe he sowed seeds in me). The hills are so steep to O'Cebreiro. Gorgeous village, and I stop for coffee. Off again. On Maps, it looks like it's 2km downhill to Triacastela. A doddle. Rain again and wind. And lots of uphill. We are in Galicia, now known for unpredictable weather. Stop twice for coffee. At the second stop, I am running out of cash. Have a sandwich and less than two euros left. Off I go. Lashing rain now. Stops. The winds are so strong. No cash point until Triacastela, and I am sure Rachelle is there.

Three more km and I am dying. See tiny Albergue. Ask for coffee (1 Euro) and ask the man to phone for a taxi for me. Terrifying ride in an old taxi with an ancient driver down a hazardous mountain road for 3km. The town looks deserted. He stops, as requested at the cash point. I spot one lonely pilgrim walking up the street, it's Rachelle. She can't believe it, nor can I. We go to her Albergue, and I insist on celebrating with a bottle of wine across the road in a café. Then Peter joins us. Then Chris, then we meet beautiful Sorin, Romanian, aged 27. Crazy David's short shorts show up too, but we manage to escape him. Have a long conversation with Antonia in the Albergue laundry - she has no English. Sleep really well.

How many coffees can one woman drink in a day? Mum's journey read like a caffeinated sprint, filled with chance meetings, taxi rescues, and joyful reunions. Mine, by contrast, was a strange cocktail of elevation, wine, and sudden grief.

Before bed, Ilze sent me a message—a simple Tibetan proverb: "The secret to a long life is: eat half, walk double, laugh triple, and love without measure." Timeless, effortless wisdom sent at just the right moment.

TINY PILGRIM TRUTH

Some days crack you open just wide enough for the light to slip in through laughter, through loss, and through the kindness of a message when you need it most.

CHAPTER 32

EVERY STEP FORWARD, EVERY NOTE LEFT BEHIND

September 29th - Day 28: Triacastela to Sarria (25 km)

I took the long route today, hoping that because all the crowds start at Sarria, they might also choose the short path.

I started in the dark with Lilia, our footsteps soft and steady, but soon enough, the morning light lured me into my own pace. I spent most of the day walking alone on a day so lovely and through a countryside so beautiful it seemed intentionally designed to stop you mid-step. The grass was impossibly green, the sky a kind of defiant blue, and the rivers offered just enough wet grass for a weary backside and a moment of quiet that wasn't trying to be profound.

Every step was taking me closer to home — both geographically and, in some curious way, internally too. But already I was questioning how I'd reconcile these two lives: the one with schedules, traffic, and to-do lists, and this one where life is measured in kilometers, coffee stops, and the simple miracle of moving forward. How do you return to the speed of emails when your heart is still tuned to the pace of footsteps? More to the point — what pieces of this life could I protect and carry home, like contraband wisdom?

Mum had chosen this longer route too, and in true form had gone even further, clocking an extra five kilometers beyond Sarria to Barbadelo. She always liked to outwalk the competition, even if the only person keeping score was herself. She doesn't remember the specifics now, thanks to the haze of Alzheimer's, but when I bring it up, she says she remembers. Or pretends she does. I still see the light in her eyes, like a movie projector; the stories dance across her face for a moment. And even after she forgets, I like to think her legs will still remember. Somewhere deep in the memory of the muscle, the Camino will live on.

I stopped in Samos for coffee and a croissant, and what a stop it was. Samos is beautiful, all winding riverbanks and ancient stone, anchored by the grand Benedictine Monastery of San Julián de Samos. Founded in the sixth century, it's a hulking reminder of the days when men built things to outlast them.

By the time I reached the little glamping site I'd booked just outside of Sarria, the sun was stretching its legs for the evening. The site was charming—think rustic chic meets safari chic. Ruth and Lilia were already there, halfway through lunch. I grabbed a beer and plopped down next to them. I'd invited Ilze to share my tent. She was still visibly rattled from the tragedy on the mountain, and some familiar company felt like the least I could offer.

Then came Sarria — the unofficial Disneyland of the Camino. If you want your Compostela certificate but can't stomach weeks of blisters and existential crises, you start here. Walk the final 100 kilometers, collect your stamps, and voilà — spiritual achievement unlocked. Sarria is a blend of medieval allure and modern pilgrim pragmatism. Its steep stone staircases, the Escalinata Mayor, lead up to the old quarter, while its cafés, pharmacies, and hostels cater to the wide-eyed and well-shod.

That evening, we gathered a lively crew for dinner: Hette, Joanna, Olivier, Ruth, Lavanya, Lilia — plus Ole, the friend of the Danish man, Henrik, who'd died on the mountain. Ilze had made sure he wasn't alone, helping him find accommodation in Sarria, walking with him, ensuring grief didn't swallow him whole. Over wine and warm plates, he shared that one of his late friend's final observations had involved me. Apparently, when I passed them at lunch that afternoon on the mountain, Henrik declared, "Now I can die happy. I've just seen the best legs on the Camino."

I replied, "Well, I have just walked 750 km; they'd better be award-winning." We laughed. There's something sacred in laughter that stitches cracks in grief, even if just for a moment.

Mum's Journal

Set off early with Rachelle and Sorin. The walk was beautiful—fog everywhere, like stepping into heaven. Met a very nice Irish couple from Mullingar, Bridie and John. A few coffee stops. Still had energy in Sarria, so we decided to push on to Barbadelo. All uphill! But we found a gorgeous private Albergue—15 euros each for a room with three beds and a fabulous bathroom. Laundry was done for us. Lovely dinner, and in bed by 10 p.m. Slept like a log. Feels like normal life again.

That line — "feels like normal life again" — caught me. What was normal now? Was it this stripped-back version of existence where all you need is a path, a place to sleep, and the occasional pastry? Or was it normal back home, with its speed, noise, and obligations? I wasn't sure anymore.

Watching Ilze care for Dani's friend reminds me of the quiet acts of service that shape our lives in ways we don't always register. These gestures—these almost invisible stitches of humanity—are the stuff life is made of.

It brought me back to my 30th birthday. Mum had planned a trip to Paris, my first. She orchestrated every detail like a producer staging the perfect debut — sunset walks along the Seine, getting gloriously lost in Montmartre, dinner inside the Eiffel Tower, a cheeky night at the Moulin Rouge. She told me, "I wanted your first time in Paris to be with someone who'd always love you more than anyone else ever could." It was magic.

Then there were her notes—tiny letters she'd slip under my pillow when I was a kid, counting kisses for every day she'd be away. Later, she upgraded to stealthily planting them in my suitcase when I visited home, ensuring I'd find them when the homesickness kicked in.

I carried that tradition forward with my own kids—these small, ordinary acts that accumulate into something extraordinary.

As I lay under the canvas of my glamping tent that night, the stars wheeling above Sarria, I felt it deeply: life is less about the kilometers we've clocked and more about the special moments we share and the memories we create.

And sometimes, it really is about taking the long route—just to make sure you don't miss any of it.

TINY PILGRIM TRUTH:

Family isn't always who you came with. Sometimes it's who holds your hand when the road gets steep.

CHAPTER 33

WHERE THE CAMINO MAGIC FOUND ME

September 30 - Day 29: Sarria to Portomarín (22.7 km)

I left Sarria at the leisurely hour of 7:30 a.m., practically a sleep-in by Camino standards. Ilze stayed behind, opting for a shorter stroll today, and we would not meet again until Santiago. I braced myself for the infamous "last 100 km crowd." I'd heard the rumors: pilgrims-by-the-busload arriving fresh-faced and impeccably clean, aiming to tick the Camino off their bucket list with just enough miles to get their certificate. But hearing about it and seeing it are two very different things. Seeing it was a bit like turning up to a quiet dinner party only to find it's now a music festival.

First, I'll admit, the intrusion grated slightly. The stillness, the space, the invisible threads that connected those of us who had walked weeks together all felt suddenly diluted. But then it struck me: maybe this was my "Camino" pop quiz before the final exam—the messy reintegration back to real life. Could I hold onto the peace I'd cultivated even in the face of chaos?

Not long after, I bumped into Ed at a café, and we decided to walk together. Our pace was interrupted shortly after by a brigade of Spanish schoolkids on a week-long Camino tour. Their charm was undeniable, and they were eager to practice their English, brimming with energy and somehow still polite. "If this is the future of Spain," I thought, "the country is in good hands." Ed groaned, as most did, about my "Camino pace," which was not quite a sprint but not sightseeing speed either. I preferred to think of it as "purposefully unhurried."

I had wisely pre-booked a hostel given the influx, but when I peeked at it, the place looked... less "rustic" and more "biohazard." Ed, ever the optimist without a bed, suggested we explore alternatives. Serendipity smiled, and the very first hotel over the river had one room left. I insisted he take it, as I had a backup, after all, but chivalry (and his stubbornness) prevailed. The room was mine.

After a glorious shower, I went hunting for a memorable meal. I struck gold just steps away and texted Ed, still feeling a twinge of guilt about the room. He had lucked out with another place and promptly asked if he could join me. After lunch, I meandered through town, where Portomarín revealed its magic.

Here's a tidbit of history: Portomarín isn't in its original spot. The town was literally moved in the 1960s, stone by stone, when a new reservoir was built and the old town was submerged. The iconic Roman bridge? Still standing proud, a testament to defiant architecture and maybe a little Spanish stubbornness.

I crossed that bridge, journaling in the sun, when I spied fishermen nearby. Ever the linguist-in-training, I consulted my

Duolingo and tried to ask, "What are you fishing for? And can you swim here?" My accent must have been Oscar-worthy because the fisherman launched into an enthusiastic monologue that left me nodding "Sí, sí" like an eager bobblehead until he realized my Spanish peaked at "hola."

The good news: swimming was allowed, and I was determined to take my first Camino dip. A quick text to the Camino crew, and within minutes, Ed, Tim, Olivier, Joanna, and Theo joined. Tim, ever the MVP, brought a six-pack.

As the sun began to bow out for the day, a handful of us—Tim, Ed, Theo, and I—plunged into the icy and gooey river, emerging breathless and alive. We perched on the banks, beers in hand, the sunset casting everything in gold. And then something happened. Not a lightning bolt, no celestial choir, but a shift, deep and cellular. Like every single cell in my body had a smiley face emoji on it.

I felt light. Free. Childlike. Joyful in a way I hadn't felt in decades, or possibly ever.

Maybe every step was a breadcrumb to this exact feeling. I wanted to bottle it. I wanted to gift it. I wanted everyone to feel this alive.

That night, I reunited with the gang in a streetside café for drinks, but dinner service was pure chaos. Starving, Ed and I peeled off to revisit our lunch spot where, mercifully, there was a table. We ate well, the perfect punctuation to a perfect day.

Before bed, I wandered back to the bridge alone to whisper my thanks to the day, to the Camino, to whatever magic was afoot. My journal entry ended: "Couldn't be happier."

Mum's Journal

Slept late, breakfast of sorts. Set off with Rachelle and Sorin. It's the last couple of days on the Camino. I am so keen to see Santiago, but I don't want the Camino to end. So beautiful, this walk. Woods, plains. Many tiny villages. So much fun. Made it to Portomarin. Gorgeous, very high bridge across the shallow river and many steep steps to climb to the village. In the village, Antonio yells, "Welcome." En route to the Albergue, Carlos invites us for a drink. He phones for places for us. Later, I buy drinks, and the numbers grow: Eric, Ed, Peter, Al. Eric invites us to dinner in the hostel at 7 p.m. Carlos comes to help me buy a new T-shirt and some wine. It's a wonderful, fun dinner. I couldn't be happier.

There it was, the same words, written twelve years apart: "Couldn't be happier."

When I read her journal that night, something inside me cracked open. I had felt her presence many times on this journey, but here in Portomarín, it was as if she was with me, as me. We shared this day, these moments, this joy.

This was the Camino's ultimate gift: not the arrival in Santiago, but the realization that happiness—that unburdened, wild, childlike happiness—was already inside me. It had just been waiting for the clutter to clear.

I didn't need the Camino to find it again. I just needed to remember that it was there, like a favorite song I'd forgotten how to hum. And now, I'll never forget. What was left to discover on this walk?

TINY PILGRIM TRUTH:

Happiness doesn't always arrive in grand gestures. Sometimes, it shows up in a cold river, a warm sun, and the quiet certainty that you've landed exactly where you need to be.

CHAPTER 34

WHEN THE RAIN DOESN'T DROWN THE SPIRIT

October 1 - Day 30: Portomarín to Palas de Rei (24 km)

I set off alone in the dark and mist, just me and my thoughts, after what had become my Camino breakfast of champions — fresh jugo de naranja. It was silent and still, the kind of quiet that feels less like loneliness and more like a secret you've been let in on. There were two ways out of town; I chose the conventional path, crossing the bridge and embracing the emptiness. No pilgrims were in sight, and admittedly, it was a little eerie. My hunch was that these new crowds were 8 am types, while I was now proudly in my pre-dawn weirdo era.

It rained. Then it poured. Then it mocked me with more rain. Luckily, every few kilometers, a village café appeared like a mirage, complete with caffeine and croissants.

As I neared one such oasis, I spotted Ruth hobbling toward me, clearly in pain and limping. Shin splints. Bad ones. But with so few days left, she was on the "just power through" plan, otherwise known as "completely bonkers." She needed fuel, fast, but the line inside was massive. Luckily, I spied Adam near the front, slipped him a fiver, and whispered to tack on an extra coffee, orange juice, and croissant. For a mere five euros, Ruth's face lit up like Christmas morning.

A few kilometers later, I found a tiny, empty café with just the owner and two gorgeous dogs. Heaven. But when I got back on the road and found Ruth again, I decided to stay by her side. We walked the rest of the way together, chatting easily. Her English was excellent, her stories better, and we laughed the way only two rain-soaked pilgrims with wrecked legs and caffeine jitters can—loud, ridiculous, and beautifully unbothered.

We arrived, drenched, in Palas de Rei, which translates to "Palace of Kings." There was no grandeur here, unless your idea of regal is a pharmacy and a few weathered cafés. But the name nods to the town's medieval past when it was said to have hosted royalty passing through on the Camino. Like much of Galicia, its stones hold stories, even if the palaces themselves have long since disappeared.

After a pharmacy pit stop (razor, because my legs had crossed into Sasquatch territory), I arrived at my quaint pension. The owner recommended a little local spot for dinner, which he said was more like eating in someone's living room than in a restaurant. I invited Lilia, her husband, Tim, and Ruth to join. The food was humble but delicious, and the conversation was even better.

Post-dinner, Tim, our perpetual enabler, convinced us to grab a final beer at a sports bar airing the Barcelona match. It was a very un-Camino kind of night, with neon lights, loud commentary, and fried snacks, but the Camino teaches you that the unexpected is always part of the path.

I was in bed by 9:30, grateful for my $20 Amazon poncho that once again saved the day. Rain was in the forecast again for tomorrow, but at least I'd be dry(ish) and slightly less hairy.

Mum's Journal

Set off with Rachelle, Sorin, and Carlos. Long, hilly road out of the village. Carlos pushes me up the steep bits. Pit stops are frequent. The route is long, but the fun makes it feel easier. We lose Sorin somewhere along the way. Exhausted when we reach the Albergue — it's sweltering. I opt for a separate dorm to secure a lower bunk. I lose track of the others but have a drink in the village and meet Peter, who seems to be losing his mind. He just can't hack the hardship. He was normal before. We go for a drink—that revives him a bit. Then we meet Al. Dinner with Carlos, others, and a Frenchman who wasn't too fond of me because he thought I crossed the Camino without my bag. I wish! All good. I slept like a log.

I spent much of today thinking about parenting: how I was raised, how I'm raising my two, and how much of this thing we all just… figure out as we go. Ruth and I chatted about it, but even after the conversation ended, the thoughts kept swirling.

My parents weren't perfect. Whose are? But I was loved, truly loved, and there was always adventure, always curiosity, even if their marriage didn't always survive the sharp rocks of their differences. I wonder who they might've been, who we might've been if they'd done the hard work on themselves. If they'd carried less pain, could they have been better parents?

I think about my own parenting, and I know I can be better. Less impatient. Less sharp around the edges on the days when life feels heavy. Parenting is the most rewarding, yet the most confronting job we'll ever have. The best any of us can do is build on the good we were given, vow to do less of the damage and to keep doing the work on ourselves.

Mel Robbins said it perfectly: "People can only meet you where they've met themselves." If my parents had met themselves more deeply, maybe they could've met us differently, too.

Still, I was lucky. I was loved—loved deeply by both and adored by my mum. And even on days when the rain won't quit and the path feels endless, that love is an umbrella all its own.

TINY PILGRIM TRUTH:

Some days you lead, some days you follow. And some days, the real grace is in choosing to slow down so that no one walks alone.

CHAPTER 35

RIBADISO REVERIE — THE NIGHT I DIDN'T KNOW I NEEDED

October 2 - Day 31: Palas de Rei to Ribadiso (24 km)

I headed out at 6:30 a.m., wrapped in darkness and yet another Spanish downpour. By now, I knew better than to whine. Complaining about rain on the Camino is like complaining about sand at the beach: utterly futile and vaguely ridiculous. Still, for a country that sells itself on sunshine and sangria, Spain was really leaning into its "Noah's Ark" era.

The 24 km flew by through mostly woodland, farms, and quiet countryside. Despite this being where the Camino del Norte and Camino Primitivo merge with the Francés, it didn't feel crowded. Proof that the early bird doesn't just catch the worm; it also dodges the walking tour buses.

Ribadiso is a gem of a village perched by the Rio Iso, barely more than a cluster of stone buildings and a bridge, but what it lacks in size it makes up for in charm. I was drenched to the bone, so arriving at my pre-booked hotel, the only hotel, felt like winning the Camino lottery. It was quaint, spotless, and (bless them) had a laundry service for 5 euros. I gladly threw in every stitch of clothing I owned and took a shower so long I'm pretty sure I set back Spain's water conservation efforts by a week.

Once scrubbed and human again, I crossed the street to a little bar where I found Ed and Adrian mid-lunch. Over the next couple of hours, the rest of our ragtag crew—Oliver, Theo, Ruth, Tim, and Joanna—trickled in. I produced a deck of cards, and before long, we were playing poker, 21, and, God help me, doing shots. I hadn't done shots in years, but somehow the Camino makes bad decisions sometimes feel like good traditions.

Somewhere between the third game and the second shot, I felt something shift again. The air felt softer. Laughter felt rounder.

The solitude I'd craved at the start wasn't what I needed anymore. Somewhere along the miles, the quiet had done its job. Now I was craving connection, warmth, the kind of camaraderie that can only be forged in shared blisters, shared rain, and shared bad decisions made in good company.

And I noticed something else: a return to softness. Years in tech had toughened me up, made me sharper, more guarded. On the outside, I looked every bit the woman, but inside I'd built walls to survive. Out here, step by step, the Camino was stripping that hardness away. I was remembering how to be soft again. Not weak, just whole. A quiet return to my femininity and to myself.

Mum's Journal

Set off really early. I wanted to be alone, heading up through the woods in the dark. It was difficult to find the path sometimes—really pitch dark, but magnificent when the light finally appeared. I hardly met a soul. I needed coffee, but it was hard to find. I pushed on and met Sorin in Melide for lunch. Carlos and Rachelle joined us. They wanted to shop; I walked on. A gallop now towards Ribadiso. I stopped too long at a gorgeous garden café. I met loads. I think I've only 3 km left—but I keep going and going and eventually reach a village that says I still have 4 km to go. I nearly die. Half dead, I get to this tiny hamlet on the river and collapse into the Albergue. I can't find my papers—Al comes to my rescue. There's a lovely garden bar behind the field where I have drinks with Rachelle and Sorin, then dinner with them. Carlos has gone ahead to Arzúa.

Reading Mum's journal tonight, I smiled as I thought about us both, twelve years apart, basking in the Camino's social heartbeat in this tiny riverside village.

I could feel her joy even through her characteristically sparse words. She was alive here among the strangers who became her tribe, in the gardens where the wine was cheap and the laughter unfiltered. Here, she didn't have to sit with the darkness she carried, the things she'd never confront. She could just be, surrounded by others, chasing light instead of shadows.

That's where our Caminos diverged. Hers was a glorious, heart-filling escape; mine has been a relentless excavation. She ran, and I don't say that as a criticism, just a truth. She ran from what she didn't want to face, while I came here to look it dead in the eye: her illness, my grief, the tangle of feelings I didn't know how to name until my feet had walked far enough to find them.

I'm not running. I came here to find the best parts of myself that had gotten buried under responsibility, pain, and pretending to be fine. I came to acknowledge the parts that weren't serving me or anyone else and to finally decide to do better. To live better.

And tonight, with clean clothes, warm food, and laughter that glowed, I felt it. I felt her. I felt myself. And it was enough.

TINY PILGRIM TRUTH:

Magic doesn't arrive on schedule. It shows up in poker games, wet socks, and the company you didn't know you needed.

CHAPTER 36

THE TOWN THAT TOOK OUR BREATH AWAY (LITERALLY)

October 2 - Day 33: Ribadiso to O'Pedrouzo (20.1km)

I somehow peeled myself out of bed early, which felt borderline miraculous given the tequila-fueled poker night we'd survived. Even more miraculously, Ed was up and ahead of me on the trail, though his gait had the air of a man in deep negotiation with his own choices. The rain had returned like a clingy ex, and yet, with my poncho, my sodden Tevas, and a spirit as buoyant as my saturated socks, I was euphoric. Cloud nine. Higher, even.

The trail lifted us under archways of eucalyptus trees, their leaves slick and glistening like nature's own stained glass. We climbed steadily out of Ribadiso, the smell of wet earth everywhere, when we hit Arzúa a few kilometers in. Breakfast was the usual croissant, coffee, and orange juice, but somehow it never lost its magic. Maybe it was the ritual; maybe it was just the relief of the warm café after the cold rain.

Like clockwork, our bedraggled crew stumbled in, one

after the other, looking like a wet cast of "Les Misérables": Tim, Ruth, Theo, Joanna, Olivier, and Adam. We laughed, ordered more coffee, and for a brief moment, the Camino felt less like a pilgrimage and more like a sitcom that had finally found its rhythm.

Beyond Arzúa, the rain persisted, but I barely noticed. The path carried us through oak woods, across streams, and though I was drenched, I was light—like the rain couldn't quite soak through to my joy.

Arriving in O'Pedrouzo was… confronting. The town greeted us with a stench so powerful I was half-convinced something had died in protest of the local plumbing. The deeper I walked, the worse it got. It was as if the entire sewage system had just thrown in the towel. Everyone seemed quieter than usual. Maybe it was reverence. Or maybe we were all just trying not to inhale too deeply.

My pension, pre-booked with such naïve optimism, turned out to be a boxy, modern eyesore with a room so tiny it felt like sleeping in Tupperware. And hot—suffocatingly hot. My options were to suffocate with the windows closed or open them and let "Eau de Municipal Despair" waft in. In this real-life choose-your-own-adventure, I opted for a shower and escape.

I found salvation in the form of a Mexican restaurant, and to my delight, the whole gang was already there. I hadn't realized how much I'd missed tacos until that moment. Tacos, margaritas—a staple in San Diego. It felt like a little taste of home on foreign soil. Conversation flowed, laughter echoed, and we made loose plans to meet again for dinner.

Later, Joanna, Lavanya, and I wandered the town, which, let's be honest, didn't take long. A few shops, a few cafés, and that persistent smell. In a tiny boutique, I bought them each a simple bracelet, a Camino shell threaded on a string as a memento of the road we'd shared. Their gratitude was disproportionate to the price but perfectly matched to the sentiment.

By the time dinner rolled around, pizza this time, the energy had shifted. Not worse, just... quieter. Thinner. Maybe 32 days of walking do that to you. Or maybe we were all beginning to grieve the ending before it arrived.

I announced my plan to leave in the middle of the night, just as Mum had, and arrive in Santiago for sunrise. No one leapt at the idea. Fair, really. But Ed, ever the gallant, insisted on joining. He didn't like the idea of me trekking through dark forests alone. And while part of me thought I should do this last stretch solo, I remembered Mum didn't walk it alone either. So I decided to let the Camino, as always, unfold the way it wanted to.

I headed back to my stifling little room, set my alarm for 2 a.m., and tried to sleep. Tomorrow, Santiago awaited.

Mum's Journal

It's just so much fun, sometimes I forget to look around at the stunning scenery. It's the second last day. I want to see Santiago. I have walked nearly 850km in its direction, always seeing the spires in my mind's eye. I just don't want the fun with this crowd to end. I don't want the lovely loneness, while not being alone, to end. Great fun with Al, Rachelee, Carolos and Sorin. Met Sorin at breakfast. Both of us wish to walk alone. I set off. Tough uphill to Arzua village. Get cash. Set off through the woods. Carlos, Eric, and Ed join me and won't go on without me. I stop at the first village for coffee. Carlos, who almost never wants coffee, stops with me despite my protests. Ed and Eric walk on. There are a lot of people on the

Camino today. Carlos and I gallop along and pass out everyone we see. I have loads of energy. Santiago is ahead. Just one more night. One village out, at Santa Irene, Carlos and I stop and he insists on buying me lunch. We stop until Sorin and Rachelle appear and all set out on our last night together (I thought) in Arca.

Met Ringrose (who used to live in Oranmore, Galway) and his barrister friend en route. Great fun. Carlos finds us a hostel. Shower, do our washing and head out for a drink. Have a great dinner. Carlos, Sorin, Al, Rachelle. A few others join us. As we leave the restaurant, I say it's such a beautiful night, maybe we should walk to Santiago. Rachelle is very enthusiastic. We had often talked about sleeping out one night – just for the ridiculous experience. The guys are laughing. I say we are serious. Then they say that if we want to go, they will come with us. So it is. Back to the hostel. Pack our bags, the number of lights we have between us (3) and to the amazement of other pilgrims, set out for Santiago.

It is a night like never before. Calm, huge moon, endless stars. Through the forest. Open fields. Across the roads. Al, who is leading, has had a glass or two of wine more than the rest of us, so I correct him on his directions many times!! We pass an airport and see a plane taking off just beside us.

I think of Brierley's book warning us of the hordes going into Santiago on the last day – lots of tourists come and realize what I so much wanted, this crazy midnight flight. Al says his bag is very heavy and we need to see some of the food he is carrying. We sit in a village, on church steps and eat cakes and biscuits. Away we go, fortified and happy. We have no plan as such. I thought we might camp out (without a tent!) up on Monte de Gozo – high on the hill, 5km outside of Santi-

ago. Lots of tourists and pilgrims stay here before leaving early in the morning. But 2 or 3 km before, there, Soring hurts his knee and is limping. Carlos wants to find a place for the night. All closed. We get into one, no one about, and I want to sleep in a kind of lounge. No seconder to this one. I empty my backpack looking for a bandage for Sorin's knee (and lose all my makeup in the search) and we push on. Cold, wet and tired, we head downhill for 5km, it seems more, into Santiago. Now what? We have no plan.

Carlos sees an Alberque. It's closed, but it has a covered patio and toilets that are open. We decide to stay. Carlos, being Spanish and at home) just can't. He's undecided. We get our sleeping bags out and lie on the cold ground. There is one covered seat long enough to lie on, but very narrow. Not wide enough to lie on its back. It is offered to me, the senior, and I gladly accept. I take out my bin bag and wrap it around me (don't get in). Carlos can't do it, so he kisses Rachelle and me goodnight (or good morning), and heads off. It must be 4 am. I think we sleep a bit. I wake up first. Frozen. It's 6am. Al wakes up, astonished at first by his surroundings, and then laughs. Sorin wakes up laughing. Rachelle is like a victim of laughing gas. We clean up as best as possible and frozen and starving head in search of breakfast. We have walked 44km in 24 hours. We really, really appreciate our coffee, toast and orange juice. Don't know where Carlos is, so head into Santiago – another 4km trek – arriving around 8 am.

I can scarcely believe that I made it. Here we are. Nearly 900km. Exhausted, Raggy looking, but so happy. We go for our certificate. We want our proof. Come back and stare at the Cathedral de Santiago again. An odd person comes in. We were so early, having walked all night. Eventually later, we see Carlos and Eric. Kisses, hugs, everyone who makes it is so happy. Am so glad to have people to share it with. I am staying in the Parador and want to make the noon pilgrim mass. Others go to find the Hostel. I can't get a seat at the Mass, and don't enjoy it that much anyway, but later the gang comes to the Parador for me and we have dinner. So nice to see them again.

All joined me in the Parador for drinks. Pure Bliss.

And just like that, Mum's account was ahead of mine, and her Camino was over before mine. For the first time, I read her next steps before walking them myself. Somehow, it felt exactly as it should—as though she was passing me the baton.

I laughed reading her words. Of course, she was the instigator of that midnight adventure. Of course, it was her. Sixty-eight years old, and she was still the one coaxing others into joy and mischief. That was her spirit: irrepressible, cheeky, and magnetic.

I'd lived that version of her all my life: midnight feasts as a child, handwritten notes slipped downstairs begging for snacks, answered every time; the French can-can she orchestrated (and starred in) at my 21st birthday; dressing up for the Galway Races; skiing in Aspen; cocktails in Vegas; theater in London; ambling in Prague; schnitzels in Berlin; hiking in Yosemite; singing in New York on New Year's Eve. A life of memories, laughter, and love.

Reading her journal now, on the eve of my own arrival in Santiago, I saw the gift she had given me more clearly than ever: the gift of a mother who loved me fully, who lived loudly, and who showed me the world wasn't just to be survived but devoured with glee.

Yes, her disease is cruel. But her life was rich, and I was the living proof of it. Her energy, her spark—they were alive in me. I carried them with me, just as I carried her.

And tomorrow, as I crossed into Santiago, I knew I'd be walking with all of her legacy, my grief, and our shared spirit.

Because this wasn't just the end of the Camino; it was the long walk home—to myself, to her, to everything that still lives in me.

TINY PILGRIM TRUTH:

Some inherit heirlooms. But lucky me, I inherited midnight walks, spontaneous plans, and a belief that life is better when you say "yes" to the ridiculous.

CHAPTER 37

WE ARRIVE AS PILGRIMS, WE LEAVE AS DANCERS

October 3- Day 33: O'Pedrouzo to Santiago de Compostela (20 km)

Here we go. The final leg. I barely slept, too restless and too wired, and got up in the inky darkness, determined to keep my promise: to reach Santiago around 8 a.m., just like Mum did.

Outside, it was misty and still, the kind of peaceful that makes you feel like the world was built just for you and this one morning. Ed was waiting, his headlamp cutting through the dark, his pale Irish legs in shorts boldly claiming their place under Spanish streetlights. Aside from the two of us fools, the town was asleep.

We set off, talking sometimes and walking in companionable silence at other times. Ed was, at times, graciously following my lead, knowing this last night was sacred for me. I knew, too, it was special for him. How could it not be? After all, this was the finale: the end of 850 kilometers, the first pilgrimage of my life, and possibly the most extraordinary thing I'd ever done on foot.

We reached Monte do Gozo — the Hill of Joy — the traditional first glimpse of the Santiago Cathedral's spires. Pilgrims for centuries have stood here, overcome with emotion at the sight of their destination. But not us. We saw mist, mist, and more mist. Still, the symbolism wasn't lost on me: sometimes you don't need to see the destination to know it's there.

As we descended, the city slowly revealed itself. The gray industrial outskirts gave way to narrow cobbled streets, stone buildings leaning gently in like old friends. The sky finally cracked open, and after days of gray, the sun emerged as if the universe had been holding its breath just for this welcome.

We stopped for breakfast and got our final pilgrim stamp from a street vendor, and it was my favorite yet, embossed and ornate. Then, we turned a corner, and there it was: the Cathedral of Santiago de Compostela, rising before us like something out of a dream.

I stood there, rooted, my eyes stinging and my heart thundering. We'd done it. We had arrived. No fanfare, no crowds. Just us, standing in the stillness of a square that has greeted pilgrims for over a thousand years.

Santiago de Compostela isn't just any city. Legend has it that the remains of Saint James the Apostle lie beneath the Cathedral, making it one of the most important pilgrimage destinations in the world alongside Rome and Jerusalem. The city's name itself comes from Sant Iago (Saint James), and Compostela is thought to mean "field of stars," a nod to the Milky Way that guided medieval pilgrims.

We just stood there, staring, and then hugged—the kind of

hug that acknowledges every step, every doubt, and every mile behind us.

Across the square was the Parador, the historic Hostal dos Reis Católicos, a former royal hospital turned hotel that has been offering pilgrims shelter since the 15th century. I was overjoyed that Ilze would soon arrive to share it with me. Charles, her boyfriend who had passed, had stayed in this very Parador on his own Camino. She always joked that Charles sent me to find her, that I reminded her of him. Maybe that was true. I like to think so.

According to my Samsung watch, I hadn't just walked 850 kilometers — I'd crossed the 1,000 km mark. Across a country on foot. No responsibilities. No calendar alerts. Just my feet, my heart, a map, and time. A rare kind of freedom, the kind that rebuilds you.

After breakfast, we collected our Compostela certificates, the proof of our pilgrimage. Then we stayed in the square, waiting for our Camino family to arrive. There were cheers, tears, and hugs. Ilze arrived last and was radiant and emotional, and just when she thought it couldn't get more overwhelming, her Dutch brothers appeared, masks on, having secretly traveled from the Netherlands to surprise her. Her joy was palpable—grief, love, and wonder colliding all at once.

Later, after showers and transformations via the Zara outfits we'd picked up in Leon. On the outside, we looked different: clean, put-together, almost unrecognizable from the dusty pilgrims we'd been just hours before. But the real transformation was underneath. A quiet, steady knowing that we'd been changed, cell by cell, step by step. We wore those clothes, but we carried the Camino stitched into our skin, into the softening of our hearts, into the way we would now move through the world. We met Ilze's brothers and Ed for drinks at the Parador bar, then dinner at a beautiful restaurant arranged by the concierge. Hetty joined, and we laughed so much, my stomach hurt.

That night, Ilze, Ed, and I toured the Cathedral by night. It was quiet, reverent, and hauntingly beautiful. The next morning, the rain returned—fitting, really. The Camino had to remind us it wasn't done with us just yet. Still, I made it to the noon Pilgrim Mass, less for religion and more for ritual.

As the Botafumeiro, the great incense thurible, swung across the cathedral's vaults, filling the air with scent and ceremony, I felt it: I was now part of this long, unbroken chain of pilgrims stretching across centuries. I had walked in their footsteps, and now Santiago was part of me, too.

That evening, I had drinks with Ruth, Tim, Carolina, Joanna, and Paulina at a tapas bar for our last hurrah. I was flying home the next day to Galway for an early 80th birthday celebration for Mum. The others were heading on to Finisterre, the end of the world, but for me, Santiago was my end, just like it was for Mum.

I walked Ruth home, tipsy and happy, then soaked in one last luxurious night in the Parador. The next morning, Ruth was gone; Ilze left shortly after. She gifted me a necklace, simple and beautiful, and hugged me, calling me her "Camino little sister." I knew we would stay connected.

The rest of the crew—Ed, Tim, Theo, Adrian, Carolina, Joanna, Paulina, Adam—gathered one last time in the Parador lobby, ponchos on, ready to brave five more stormy days to Finisterre. We hugged. We laughed. We promised to stay in touch.

And then, right there in the rain-soaked square, before the Cathedral of Santiago de Compostela, they danced.

That was the Camino.

It doesn't just take you across a country; it teaches you to dance.

"PILGRIM'S LAST TRUTH"

The Camino ends in a city called Santiago de Compostela, which means "Field of Stars." But the real destination wasn't on any map. It was a feeling—a feeling I want to leave you with today: **every cell in my body had a smiley face emoji on it.** And that place of joy? It's not at the end of a road in Spain. It's a geography that exists inside you, and it's only ever a few brave steps away.

CHAPTER 38

THE PEOPLE SHE CARRIED (AND WHO CARRIED HER BACK)

I thought I was walking the Camino to find my mother. I didn't realize the path would also deliver her whole and brilliant, through the people who loved her. Not just on the trail, but after it. In email threads, in surprise reunions, in a phone call when a heart had broken and somehow, she talked them back into themselves again. In bike rides on Le Canal du Midi, in laughter in Salamanca, in wine in Ireland, in a Spanish bridge after midnight with no bed, no plan, and absolutely no panic.

When I reached out to Mum's Camino pals to tell them she had Alzheimer's, I was bracing for sorrow. What came back was something else: joy, gratitude, stubborn hope, and story after story of my mother being exactly who I knew she was and more. These aren't just memories. They're proof of who she was, of how she walked, of how she loved, and of how, even now, she's still teaching me what matters.

Rachelle—"She was the heart of the group."

"What has struck me the most is your mom's ability to bring people together and make them feel included. I have so many memories of meals with her and others on the Camino, and it seems like your mom was really the heart of the group —the one who brought everyone together: her laughter, her stories, her energy."

Rachelle's words landed like a gentle truth I had always known but maybe hadn't named. My mother wasn't just a walker; she was a gatherer—the kind who makes the table bigger.

When we were kids, her parties were legendary. She'd remove all the furniture from the living room—literally drag it into the garage—because, as she put it, "If people sit, they won't mingle, they won't dance, and they certainly won't have a good time." And you know what? She was right. By the end of every party, everyone knew everyone, and everyone—even the shy neighbors—was dancing, laughing, and chatting like they had been best friends for years. Those furniture-free parties became the neighborhood highlight. My mother had this instinct for connection that was as natural as breathing.

"In 2013, we had our Camino reunion in Ireland… In 2014, your mom, Peter, and I cycled 350 km on Le Canal du Midi… In 2015, your mom, Carlos, Erik, and I met in Salamanca… In 2016, I went to Ireland again—hikes, laughs, adventures… around the time she was starting treatment for breast cancer."

The Camino didn't end in Santiago. It went on—in airports, in train stations, in borrowed bikes along a French canal, in Irish kitchens where she poured wine and stories like she'd been waiting her whole life to host strangers who had become family.

"In 2018, I was going through a hard time after a breakup. I called your mom since I knew she would cheer me up… She convinced me to fly to Ireland four days later."

Of course she did. That's my mother: zero hesitation, infinite welcome. "Come. Land here. We'll walk this bit together."

Sorin — "She touched so many of us."

"Walking the Camino with Nuala, Rachelle, and Carlos remains one of the most meaningful experiences of my life. She loved the simple rhythm—walking, sharing meals, discovering beauty in the everyday moments. Nuala is a remarkable woman, so powerful and kind, and we shared so much laughter and fun. From her, I realized that age can be just a number." She would put everything in a positive light; I remember sharing stories along the way. We even walked the last leg to Santiago, around 50 km overnight, reaching the destination in the early hours of the morning, with nowhere to find accommodation, so we had to sleep outside in our sleeping bags. She had no problem with that; it was part of the adventure. We were even joking about how simple life can be on the Camino, and one can find happiness just by having a bed to sleep in and toilet paper in the bathroom. Yet she would be so elegant and classy and invite us for a treat at the finest hotel in Santiago de Compostela. I was happy to visit her in Ireland together with Rachelle (from Canada), a couple of years after the Camino, and relive those memories. She took us around the island to so many places, being such a great host and guide.

There's such tenderness in that last line. Even now, as the

disease thins the edges of her memory, the essentials remain—walking, coffee, people. The Camino distilled to its purest form: movement, warmth, and conversation. Love, in the simplest of rituals.

"Please do share the book when it's ready. It is so nice of you to keep her story alive. She touched so many of us."

I thought I was keeping her story alive. But maybe it's the other way around—it's her story keeping me alive, reminding me to keep showing up, to keep gathering, and to make the table bigger.

Erik said, "Invite her to walk a stage with me in her imagination."

"I also remember the indescribably beautiful time on the Camino. It was 'only' one month, but this month has so much radiance for many following years… You can probably only understand this if you've walked it yourself."

He's right. It burns brighter after you leave. The Camino ages well. It doesn't go; it settles in. It changes shape and keeps showing you what it was really about—long after your blisters have forgotten they existed.

"I met Nuala again in 2015 in Madrid with Carlos and Rachelle—a very nice reunion. About the journal, I would be very happy. Please send my love to Nuala and invite her to walk a stage of the Camino with me in her imagination. I suggest we start in St. Jean Pied de Port and walk to Roncesvalles over the Pyrenees."

Carlos said, "When we looked at each other in the face, we understood."

Carlos wrote to me with a sorrow that felt old and kind and soaked in Spanish wine. He couldn't phone her—his English, her memory, both would fail them. But he reminded me that language wasn't what bound them. It was presence. It was glances. It was acts of kindness. It was laughter. It was the way she looked at you and made you feel known.

"That trip I shared with your mother will always remain in my heart… long conversations, wine, laughter, affection… I would appreciate it if you could keep me informed… I will open a bottle of wine, toast to her in my mind as we used to, and read her journal… I fear I will end up crying again when I start to remember. If you ever walk the path, although your mother is present in your feelings, it will ultimately be a beautiful experience for you, as it was for us. Take care of yourself, too."

And there it was. The lesson I didn't know I needed. Even as she forgets, my mother is still orchestrating this: people who loved her are still teaching me to mind myself, to raise a glass, to walk anyway, to let love be simple, messy, generous, and brave.

From Rachelle, I learned my mother wasn't just a pilgrim. She was a host, a node, a builder of belonging. From Sorin, I learned that the simplest things—walking, coffee, conversation—were her cathedrals. From Erik, I learned that the Camino is a time-release drug: you take it once, and it changes the rest of your life. From Carlos, I learned we don't need words when we have presence—and that some goodbyes are just invitations to remember.

And from all of them, I learned this: even as her memory fades, her impact doesn't. She is still teaching me. Even with Alzheimer's, there are lessons she imparts—be patient, be kind, and say "I love you" again, just in case they forget.

That friendship is a pilgrimage of its own. That age is just a reckless number if your spirit stays willing. That a good meal, a good laugh, and a stubborn optimism will see you over mountains.

And that love, kindness, and laughter really are all that matter—which she somehow keeps finding new ways to show me, even now.

CHAPTER 39

THE CAMINO ENDS. THE JOURNEY BEGINS

There's a moment on the Camino — not marked by any milestone or map — when you realize you're not walking toward a city, or a cathedral, or even a certificate.

You're walking yourself home.

For me, that home was not a place but a state of being I'd long forgotten. A version of me that existed before titles and targets and self-worth wrapped in LinkedIn endorsements. The me who sang at full volume without apology. The me who knew joy wasn't earned — it was remembered.

On the Camino, something magical happens. You begin as a body: blistered, stiff, protesting every incline. As your body strengthens, then the mind unclutters, the noise quiets, and finally, if you've let it, your soul cracks wide open. Wide enough to let the light back in.

I arrived in Santiago after 33 days and 1,000 kilometers underfoot. But the most extraordinary journey was the one that stretched between my ears and beneath my ribs. I walked with my mother's voice in my journal, her joy stitched into every step, her spirit—playful, fierce, unforgettable—alive again inside me.

We were two women, twelve years apart, walking the same path. One of us was fighting to hold on to memory, while the other was learning to let go.

Mum's Alzheimer's had sent me searching for her, but the Camino gave me back pieces of myself. I faced my grief, my anger, and my over-identification with a career that once defined me. It stripped me of my roles, my armor, my status, and left me raw, real, and softer—a woman who traded hard edges for open hands.

That was the true gift. I didn't walk away from my life; I walked back to it, reassembled.

People ask, "Does the Camino change you?"

It doesn't; it reveals you.

It reminds you that joy is not a fluke. It's your factory setting. That kindness, in its smallest forms—a bandaged blister, a shared orange, a stranger's smile—can change the trajectory of someone's day, maybe even their life.

It reminds you that life is really just one long walk. Some stretches are uphill. Some feel like a dance. And occasionally, you'll get caught in a monsoon and smell like a wet sock, but someone will always appear with a story, a song, or a shared beer to get you through.

When my daughter asked me how I felt when I reached Santiago, it was simple.

I told her, "Every cell in my body had a smiley face emoji on it."

I had found the place of joy inside me, and now I know I can always find my way back.

To anyone reading this: If you're lost, or stuck, or numb...

walk. Maybe not 800 kilometers, but walk somewhere new. Strip away the excess. Put one foot in front of the other. Listen to the sound of your own breath, the whisper of your soul reminding you who you've always been underneath it all.

That's what the Camino is: not an escape, but a remembering.

Of who we are. Of what matters. Of the fact that joy isn't waiting at the end of the road; it's waiting inside you, just a few steps beyond where you stopped looking.

And if you're lucky, on that road, you'll find your own reason to "dance in the rain."

Because that's the Camino. It doesn't just teach you to walk; it teaches you to dance.

And I am still dancing.

EPILOGUE

My mother now lives in a nursing home nestled in the Galway countryside close to her old home. The caretakers are wonderfully kind, and she is well taken care of. Sometimes they even let her answer the phone. She reassures patients in that steady, professional tone, telling them their X-ray will be ready soon.

Physically, she is strong. Her humor remains intact. She knows me, though at times I blur into her sister or into my sister, Barbara. She struggles more with my brothers, perhaps because the daughters orbit closer, visiting and calling. Barbara is steadfast; she takes Mum for walks, massages, manicures, or simply somewhere new, knowing stimulation matters. The smiles may fade from memory within minutes, but the joy lingers in her body's chemistry, like sunlight stored in her cells.

When I returned from the Camino, everyone said I looked years younger, lighter, and brighter. The journey shook something loose in me. It reminded me to prioritize what matters most: my health, my family, and the work that fuels me. I launched my own consulting business, travel back to Ireland every few months, and savor precious time with Mum and with Dad, who, at eighty-seven, remains fit and full of wit. I have visited Ilze in Zurich, had Ruth visit me in San Diego and walked a portion of the "Salt Path" in England with Ruth, Tim and Ed.

The Camino may have ended, but the journey continues. Every visit to Galway, every walk with Mum, every moment I choose to live with presence. One day soon, I will sit beside her and read these pages aloud. And when she looks up at me, laughing as if hearing the story for the first time, I will know we are exactly where we are meant to be.

"Letter to My Mother"

Dear Mum,

All along the Camino, I felt you with me. In the rhythm of my footsteps, I could hear your laugh; in the kindness of strangers, I saw your open heart; and in the stubborn hills, I recognized that streak of grit you passed on to me. People have always said you were warm, quick-witted, and wildly charming, and when they say I remind them of you, I know it's the highest compliment I will ever receive.

I carried your journal in my pack, but really, I was carrying you. Your words, simple, practical, sometimes funny without meaning to be, reminded me that joy is found in the small things: a café con leche, a roadside sunflower, the relief of taking your boots off at the end of the day. You taught me that life is not measured in milestones but in the moments we pay attention to.

Even now, as memory slips away like sand through your

fingers, those parts of you remain. Your humor still bubbles up, your energy still fills a room, and your instinct to care for others never left, whether it's making sure your fellow residents in the home get their imaginary "X-rays" or how you hug me when we greet with the same fierce love you always did.

From you, I learned resilience, but also tenderness. I learned how to laugh at myself, how to find faith in ordinary things, and how to keep walking, even when the way ahead isn't clear. The Camino gave me time to see all of this more clearly, to realize how deeply you've shaped me and the way I lead, the way I love, and the way I move through the world.

So thank you, Mum, for your spirit, your stubbornness, your beauty, your strength, and your kindness. But thank you mostly for your love.

Like the inscription I once wrote in a photo album of our adventures: so you could return to those moments in the absence of new ones. You are — and always will be — the closest thing to magic I will ever know. I can still hear your delighted shriek when you first read those words. No one will ever love me with the same wild completeness, the same fierce devotion. For that, and for you, I am endlessly grateful.
With love, gratitude, and laughter — always,

Your baby girl,
Andy

ABOUT THE AUTHOR

Andrea Hogan is a mother, tech marketing executive, writer, animal lover, wife and life adventurer who swapped boardrooms for backpacks after realizing the life she had built no longer fit quite right. In the thick of midlife transitions, a mother diagnosed with Alzheimer's, career crossroads, menopause, and the quiet ache that something had to change, she set out to walk 500 miles across Spain on the Camino de Santiago.

Born in Galway and now based between Ireland and California, Andrea writes with equal parts humor and heart about the messy, magical business of becoming who we are. Her debut memoir, *The Closest Thing to Magic: The Camino de Santiago – Through My Mother's Forgetting and My Own Becoming*, traces a pilgrimage taken in her mother's footsteps and within her mother's fading memories, discovering along the way how grief, reinvention, and grace can coexist.

When she's not writing, Andrea leads her consultancy, ALLWEST, helping tech companies chart their own transformations. She believes in the restorative power of yoga and hiking, style, laughter, family, friendships and a well-timed glass of wine.

Printed in Dunstable, United Kingdom

79526204R00111